VOLUME NINETEEN
The Talking Stick
Forgotten Roads

A publication of the
Jackpine Writers' Bloc

Copyright © 2010 The Jackpine Writers' Bloc
All rights reserved by the authors.
Printed in the United States by Morris Publishing®
3212 East Highway 30, Kearney, NE 68847
1-800-650-7888

Artwork from iStockphoto.com

www.jackpinewriters.com – www.thetalkingstick.com
Send correspondence to Jackpine Writers' Bloc
13320 149th Ave, Menahga, MN 56464
sharrick1@wcta.net

ISBN: 978-1-928690-14-6

Table of Contents

Table of Contents

Table of Contents

Table of Contents

Co-Editor's Note – Sharon Harris

Editor's Choice: "Levee" by Marsha C. Porter (p. 61)

My Editor's Choice this year is "Levee." This poem is probably the best expression of grief that I have ever read. It tells you how it spreads through the whole house, coloring everything, affecting everyone, changing all it touches. It just takes over. It expresses beautifully how grief overwhelms you.

So many of the other submissions for this year's book were, in general, about aging and, in particular, about Alzheimer's. So often, all an elderly person has left are their memories and the theft of them by Alzheimer's is a sad thing. My parents didn't have Alzheimer's but memories do fade as they get older. I was reminded that my dad's stories died with him. All that richness—lost. I was too busy living my own life to take time to sit down, ask him questions, and record and absorb his stories.

I am doing the best I can to record some of Mother's life. I found a book called The Story of My Life—I am sure there are many like it. She has already forgotten so much that has happened in her life. But as I went through that book and asked her questions, I was amazed that she could remember all the old relatives' names, the names of pets, even the types of flowers, bushes, and trees in their yard. Her own mom had died when my mother was only 4 or 5. Her dad was left to raise 3 young kids on his own. Their father drank a lot, but you had to give him credit. This wasn't how he expected his life to turn out either—but he did not leave them. Through his sorrow, he kept the farm going, kept the family together, milked the cows, raised crops, etc.

I remember the one thing she said that really got to me. Often, their father would take the horses and wagon to drive to town for beer. Sometimes he would be gone for a long time. She told me how she and the two other little kids would stand at the end of the driveway, out by the road, in the dark. They stood and waited and listened to see if they could hear hoof beats or the jingle of harness—so they knew Pa was finally on his way home.

Please, those of you who can, record those stories that your parents or grandparents know. Preserve those memories. My dad's are already lost and my mother's are fading fast. Record them, use them to inspire you. Don't let them disappear unspoken or unwritten.

Co-Editor's Note – Tarah L. Wolff

Editor's Choice: "Minneapolis Winter, '05" by Timothy Otte (p. 169)

I love Billy Collin's poetry, but really, who wouldn't? I hate contrite poetry that was written to sound poetic. I hate poetry that speaks to no one and nothing, not to the writer, not to the reader. Poetry must speak; it must resonate. And, to me, the best poetry is clear to understand, doesn't need poetic words or poetic forms. The best poetry is about seeing the seeds in the apple. The truth in the reality of the moment.

This is why I chose "Minneapolis Winter, '05" by Timothy Otte for my Editor's choice this year. You can literally smell the cold while you read this poem. You can feel the frost on your fingers and the too-hotness of your jacket as you continue the futile attempt to shovel the damn walk (again). I chose this poem because it is the truth. We all earn that shot of schnapps in our hot cocoa, maybe more often than we admit. And we've all had to sleep alone and, some of us too, more often than we want to admit.

The truth has been the driving force of my writing life the past few months. I started the adventure of a blog. I have a few rules for myself. Number one: always be honest. I started a blog about the process of writing my books. My tag line is: "This is about revising, working, editing, re-writing, re-thinking, re-working, and most of all this is about DOUBT."

But the truth has been a hard thing. How much truth do you give in a blog? I realized that if this blog is about me writing my books, then this blog is about my life. I couldn't just pretend I didn't have a life and just write and write and write. That would be clear and present bull crap to anyone who had ever tried to be a writer. I've found that the truth is that I can't honestly blog about my writing without admitting to the good and the bad and the ugly of what's happening in my life. Our lives fuel our writing, hinder our writing, and inspire our writing. As badly as we want to be locked in a hole somewhere just to write for six months at a time, the truth is: we write from our wounds.

The deadline, the type of writing that it requires, the fact that I must edit myself—this blog has been a good thing for my writing. If you think you might be interested in starting a blog, I suggest you try wordpress.com; it's free and it's the top-rated blogging software on the net. My blog is at tarahlynn.com.

Poetry Judge
Heid E. Erdrich

Heid E. Erdrich writes poetry, nonfiction, and drama. She has been the recipient of two Minnesota State Arts Board fellowships, awards from The Loft Literary Center and the Wordcraft Circle of Native Writers. She won the Minnesota Book Award for poetry in 2009. Heid earned degrees from Dartmouth College and the Johns Hopkins University Writing Seminars. She taught writing for many years and now serves as a visiting author at colleges and universities across the country.

Creative Nonfiction Judge
Elizabeth Jarrett Andrew

Elizabeth Jarrett Andrew is a writing instructor and spiritual director living in Minneapolis, Minnesota. She is a recipient of a Minnesota State Arts Board artists' fellowship, the Loft Career Initiative Grant, and is a Minnesota Book Awards finalist. She teaches creative writing at the Loft Literary Center, Hamline University, and various religious communities in the Twin Cities.

Fiction Judge
Nathan Jorgenson

Nathan Jorgenson grew up in Jackson, Minnesota. He attended Concordia College and U. of M. Dental School. He wrote *Waiting for White Horses* in 2004 and *The Mulligan* in 2007. He was awarded the Ben Franklin Award for Best New Voice in Fiction. Both novels were finalists for Independent Publishers Book of the Year Awards. He also writes for outdoor magazines and is an avid hunter.

The Winners - $500 Prize

Poetry Winner (p. 1)
"Night Train"
by Russell Jacobson

Russ grew up on a farm and graduated from high school in Lake Park, Minnesota. He lived in Park Rapids for 25 years and joined Jackpine Writers' Bloc in the mid '80s, moving back to Lake Park recently. He usually writes poetry and short fiction.

Creative Nonfiction Winner (p. 2)
"A Second One"
by Susan Kathleen Spindler

Susan is a lover of words, dance, music, and all other forms of art that touch and grow the soul. She is an avid golfer, swimmer, gardener, cook. She works full-time as a psychotherapist and clinical nurse specialist. She lives in Edina, Minnesota, and belongs to Ink Splots, a group of wonderful writing women.

Fiction Winner (p. 5)
"Prairie Promises"
by Barbara Marshak

Barbara is the author of *Hidden Heritage, the story of Paul LaRoche,* the biography of the award-winning Native American recording artist, Brule. *Hidden Heritage* is now a television series based on the book. Barbara has been published in *Groovy Chicks, Cup of Comfort, Talking Stick, Guideposts, Minnesota Monthly,* and *Lake Country Journal.* Barbara lives in Lakeville, Minnesota.

Second Place - $100 Prize

Second Place Poetry (p. 10)
"Police Log Poem"
by Susan Niemela Vollmer

Susan was raised in Ely, Minnesota. She and her husband have lived in Moorhead and north of Duluth. They now live in Rice Lake, Wisconsin. Her work has appeared in *Minnesota Monthly, North Coast Review, Lake Country Journal* magazine, and other publications.

Second Place Creative Nonfiction (p. 11)
"Laundry Stories: Beethoven"
by Marsha C. Porter

Marsha lives in Minneapolis, Minnesota, where she is a parent, a writer, and an art therapist. She works with the Collaborative Law Institute, providing support for those in the process of divorce. Her first book, *Take My Hand, Twelve Stories of Dissolution and Healing,* was published in 2008 under the pen name Sasha Porter Blue. She is currently working on two more collections of essays, collaborating on a journal for healing, and working on her November Novel to ready it for publishing.

Second Place Fiction (p. 14)
"South Side Spirits"
by Nicole Borg

Nicole is a poet and occasional fiction writer. Her work has appeared in *Dust & Fire, Green Blade,* and *Chantarelle's Notebook* e-zine. She lives with her husband and son in Wabasha on the lovely Mississippi.

Honorable Mention

Poetry

"North Face" by John Thornberg (p. 78)
"Vernon's White Onions" by Doris Lueth Stengel (p. 196)
"The Shape of Death" by Anne M. Dunn (p. 210)
"Hit-and-Run" by Audrey Kletscher Helbling (p. 114)
"Alzheimer's, Early Onset" by Candace Simar (p. 204)

Creative Nonfiction

"Tonight" by Dennis Herschbach (p. 129)
"The Ride Home" by Betty Hartnett (p. 175)
"Mandatory Fun" by Lyla E. Owens (p. 121)

Fiction

"The Organist" by Vern Thompson (p. 101)
"Dawn" by Niomi Rohn Phillips (p. 25)
"Ghost on the Bus" by Lindsy J. O'Brien (p. 43)
"One Side of the Vase" by Bonnie West (p. 69)

Editors' Choices

"Minneapolis Winter, '05" by Timothy Otte (p. 169)
"Levee" by Marsha C. Porter (p. 61)

VOLUME NINETEEN
The Talking Stick
Forgotten Roads

First Place Poetry by Russell Jacobson

Night Train

Gyrating eye mad in the night, an old train
screams through an unguarded crossing—
dead leaves swirling—tall grass recoiling at
its blast, bowing in its wake.

Rocking in tow, wooden box cars once
owned by hobos bear the best of a good
man's mind and most of his memory.

Relentlessly, the train races east like a clacking
ticker-tape machine—no gains, all losses onboard—
a strand of life unraveling, traveling back
through a lifetime of dawnings—perhaps taking
measure, perhaps seeking anchorage.

Without something formidable like a Model A
truck or a cable-operated crawler—something
an old train might recognize, might respect—I
am powerless to oppose it here on this country
crossing of gravel and steel—all hope but the
myth of penny on rail.

First Place Creative Nonfiction
by Susan Kathleen Spindler

A Second One

She stares at the sage green walls confining her. Hospital green. The scent of alcohol, opaque yet nudging into her consciousness, lingers. The electric bed next to her is mercifully unoccupied. The sheets, tucked and angled like angels in the military pulled linen duty. Her side faces the street. The window ledge is flanked with yellow chrysanthemums, a variegated ivy. It is the dead of January; too cold to snow. Two women with colorful scarves triple-wrapped squint against the wind and hasten toward Bruegger's.

"How are you feeling?"

Another nameless nurse who scans the monitors, wears orange Crocs.

Other than my contemplating (this would be at intervals through the night when I could not sleep because of the pain) how I could get to the nurses' station, steal your whole stash of Oxycontin, swallow it, sleep forever—I'm fine. But that I am tied to this bed by a saline IV stuck in my bruised hand, a bag displaying the contents of my emptied bladder (lucky me), and the drainage tube tied by sutures to my chest wall, I might have tried.

She notes a thrill at her silent monologue. She names it justified anger, at the IV pole and digital monitor stationed next to her like a prison guard, the tubes draped over her bed like snakes, the huge suture line that runs a transverse path across her chest wall where yesterday, she still had a left breast.

"I'm fine. What's your name?"

"I'm Gwen. The doctor will be in soon. You didn't sleep well last night. I can get the feeding tube and the Foley out so you can be more comfortable. How is the wound pain?"

Her left breast's new name: "wound." The word leaves her stunned and empty.

"I would like another Oxycontin."

Maybe Gwen does understand, at least about the physical discomfort.

She wonders how Gwen decided to work in oncology. No plausible guesses arise.

Strange, she thinks: yesterday, her life hung in a dark jeopardy until her doctor pronounced, "We got it all." Today, she wants the sacrificed part of her badly enough to turn in her life because it is gone.

She does not tell Gwen about the vision . . . or a dream? The tin scrub bucket at the end of her bed. In it, quivering and warm, a bulbous hunk of flesh, crying for her to pick it up and hold it. Her left breast. Her wound.

Martin Luther King's Day. She is free at last, to go home and get used to her body, half breastless. She reads Kubler-Ross, the stages of grief. A month passes. She notes the strange and malignant tentacles that wrapped around her heart when she first heard her diagnosis, release, slowly, their clenched grip. She visits the bra lady's shop reluctantly. A woman who has survived cancer herself works here full-time. *There are that many women who go through this? Who knew?* The woman tenderly fits her with a prosthesis. *An ugly word . . . maybe stuffing?* The woman's words and touch are gentle, compassionate. She leaves the shop with two bras, stuffing, and tears. Memories that touch evokes stick in her chest.

Three months later, Claire, her best friend since college, visits. They discuss living with two breasts vs. one, the pros and cons of reconstructive surgery, extenders, stomach or back tissue, saline or silicone. The two strive for objectivity, like deciding about a Buick or a Honda, or keeping the old clunker.

"Do you want to see it?"

"Sure," says Claire, without hesitation. "It healed well. It looks like it wants to fall into the shape of your other breast. It looks great!"

She didn't flinch, placate or cry. It feels like she still regards me as whole.

Later, over Merlot and bruschetta, she says: "It's just not time, Claire. I can't imagine wanting a second one right now."

"It's not something you have to do. Not ever, if you don't want to."

Claire really is trying to understand, as much as any two-breasted woman could.

She sits on the beach during her trip to Florida. It is one year post surgery. The cool breeze, the scent of the ocean, the loll and lap of the foamy crests, the hungry squawking cormorants that dip and loop: these give her life.

People gather on the shore in the distance. She walks toward them to investigate. A huge female leatherback turtle is on the beach. Biologists surround it, coaxing it toward the water. The fear and peril of the stranded sea animal is reflected in the anxious faces of the bystanders who keep a distance.

The turtle is lost and disoriented. It wants to move away from the shoreline. Two of the attending biologists use poles. Working gently, they wedge one behind its front flippers and one at its back. One biologist caresses its head and rubs the shell. One pours water over the turtle to keep it moist and speaks to it in soothing tones. Everyone knows this is a race against time.

Her silent prayer: *Go toward the water. You can do it!*

Later, after the turtle reenters the water and swims away, she learns the animal had been tagged in Columbia in the 1990s. She calls Claire to describe the ordeal.

"Claire, I still have goose bumps. Swimming to South America! How often in a lifetime do you get to see this?"

Never in her first lifetime. This magnificent creature, its shell mottled and gashed with life, is called by ancient instinct to navigate dangerous waters for thousands of miles, a yearly sojourn. Its sole purpose: to release the life within.

She ponders what she has seen: a turtle, lost and confused, wants to stop and let life go on without it. Caring others surround the turtle, help it. It hears life calling, reenters the ocean, resumes the journey. On life's terms. No guarantees.

She hears the calling too. And she wants it again. On its terms. No guarantees. She wants a second one.

First Place Fiction by Barbara Marshak

Prairie Promises

A strange noise stirs me, but my bones are simply too tired to move. I drift back to my dream . . . I am still in Sweden and we have yet to make our long journey to America. Elot is sitting beside me, holding my hand in his. *My sweet Corena, we will have a wonderful life in America, I promise. Here we have no hope. In America there is so much land, even a poor soul like myself can own his own farm . . . .*

The crackling sounds come again. Our cabin creaks routinely as it settles, especially on such cold winter nights. The grand white farmhouse with a pillared front porch that Elot promised is for now a primitive cabin. We have cupboards for a kitchen, a private room for Elot and me, and a loft for the older children. I sense Elot turning over and his movements awaken me further. No doubt it is time to add wood to the stove. The past seven days have been colder than I thought possible, even living in Sweden. It's our first winter at Horse Head Lake and *min godhet*, we burn wood nonstop, day and night.

A waft of smoke strikes my nose and I sniff. *Smoke.*

In an instant my eyes open, senses alert. I sit up in bed. "Elot!" I grab his shoulders and shake hard. "There's smoke!"

"Ja? Vad ar det?"

"I smell smoke, Elot! Hurry!" My bare feet hit the floorboards and I turn to the cradle next to our bed. I snatch Sadie into my arms and grab her blanket. Elot opens the bedroom door and a thunderous burst of brightness fills my view. Orange and yellow flames dance across the width of the cabin, blocking the cupboards and only door. The log wall behind the stove is engulfed in a fiery glow that roars back with danger.

I cling to the bedroom doorway, shaking, protectively pressing Sadie's face into my bosom. Elot rushes to the ladder and scrambles halfway up. "Hans! Louisa! Wake up!"

The terror in his voice pierces my eardrums, sending me into a panic. The heat is intense, tall flames pulsate in rapid, rhythmic motions forming a barricade to our only way out. "Elot! What do we do?!"

Hans and Louisa climb down the ladder and stand behind Elot. "Pa!" Hans cries. "How do we get out?"

Stricken with fear, Louisa's cries turn to screams; her blue eyes glisten with tears.

"We have to run through the flames to the door," Elot shouts. "It's the only way!"

"No!" screams Louisa. "No! I can't!"

"We can't wait, it's too late . . . . " Elot says, watching the fire consume our hand-built home.

The baby wakes and, sensing danger, begins to cry. "Shhh," I say between sobs, trying to calm her when I know the logs are too thick . . . the few windows too small.

Elot's whiskered face is covered in sweat and fear. He looks much older than his thirty-three years. "I'll take Hans and Louisa through first," he says, "and then I'll come back for you and the baby."

Louisa clings to Elot, all the while screaming, "No, Pa!" Nine-year-old Hans tries to be brave, but the raging fire is too intense and all I see is my frightened little boy.

"Give me the quilt," Elot shouts between coughs.

I reach for the wool quilt on our bed. Ma gave it to us the day we said our vows, May 1, 1861. Elot puts it around them, Hans on one side, Louisa on the other. "We must go quickly," he shouts above the fire. "Now!"

Barefoot, they race into the flames. I cover my face, unable to watch. Sobs overtake me as I clutch the door frame. Seconds later Elot is at my side, the hand-stitched quilt singed black. "Corena!" He grabs my arm and throws the quilt over us. *"Now!"*

Elot leads me forward. The heat is powerful. Instinctively I pull back. "Hold your breath!" Elot puts one arm behind me and pushes. The floorboards burn my feet. I can't hold my breath and smoke fills my lungs. I cough, blinded from the heavy quilt, burning now on top of us. Elot pushes me again and I collapse into the snow next to Hans and Louisa. The burnt remnants of our wedding quilt *hiss* against the snow bank.

Icy air fills my lungs, stinging deep inside my chest. I turn to the children, crying and shaking in the frigid night air. Elot falls to his knees, gasping for breath between gut-wrenching coughs.

"What do we do, Elot?" I ask, watching our dreams vanish into billowing smoke. All our possessions are inside, everything we lovingly carried with us to America.

"We must . . . walk to . . . Charls and Carolina . . . the lake."

"Across the lake? We are barefoot!" I say. "The snow is too deep. My feet have burns."

"We will freeze, Corena, we must get help." Elot struggles to stand. "Hans, Louisa, come. We must walk to Vedens, across the lake. Carolina will have the stove going . . . warm quilts for us. Hurry now."

Elot takes a few steps toward the lake. He cries out in pain and leans into a tree for support.

"Elot, what's wrong?"

He turns away from the children. "My feet . . . are burned too."

Light from the fire shows the blisters on Elot's feet and my gut wrenches. I try to calm the children. "Listen, listen . . . Pa will lead the way for us. Hans, you follow and hold Louisa's hand. I will be right behind you. Go now, follow Papa."

Moonlight illuminates the surrounding prairie in a bluish haze. We near the shoreline where the lake has frozen and thawed and then froze again. Jagged shards of ice cut my tender flesh. Snowdrifts rise and fall like white ribbons. Beneath us, the ice creaks in an eerie moan, momentarily halting the children's whimpers. In the distance, a wolf howls, followed by the rushing wind across the open lake.

Sadie fights me, wanting down. It takes all my strength to keep her in my arms. Louisa's shawl slips from her shoulders and I pull it up. Our thin cotton gowns are no match for the frigid January night.

The lake is long and narrow. We cross where it is the shortest distance, yet on this night it seems too far. I look back, the glow visible through the trees. Above us, heaven's stars hang in intricate lace patterns. I can no longer feel my feet or legs. Each step is difficult, laborious. Panting and breathless, the children fall and I help them up. Elot can barely walk. I can make out the darkened shape of the Veden cabin, see the smoke coming from their chimney.

One more step, Corena.

Keep going.

My mind plays tricks on me. I realize now Louisa and Hans are helping Elot. He cannot walk on his own. We reach the shore and struggle to climb over the piles of snow.

"Louisa, run to the cabin for help! Hans, help Papa!" I try to shout, but the words float softly from my throat.

Soon I hear voices. *"A kar Gud i himmel!"* Oh, dear God in heaven!

Ah, our Swedish friend, Charls Veden. We are saved.

I think of the pretty flowers that filled the wild prairie our first summer at Horse Head Lake. Elot was so proud to own land. *Eighty acres*, he said to me, *just like I promised*. He took me to the site he'd chosen for our cabin. Already a new life was fashioning within me. I picked a handful of flowers; purple ones, others pale pink, tall yellow ones, like droplets of sunshine, imagining our life in this land called *Min-ne-sota*. Elot cut the thickest trees to use for the logs, to keep us warm in the harsh winter, he said. We stayed with Elot's cousin Josephine in Parkers Prairie until our cabin was built. A difficult woman at best, she bossed me around like a servant. At first, I was afraid to move to the wilderness. I heard stories of Indians attacking settlers and the great uprising in '62. But after a summer living under Josephine's thumb, Elot couldn't finish the cabin soon enough.

Elot . . . .

My own cries wake me. Elot passed first. Charls hitched up his team and went to town to fetch Doc Hanson but it was too late. The gangrene set in and there was no chance. Charls crossed the lake the morning after the fire. In a hushed voice, he said he followed a trail of flesh the whole way.

Hans and Louisa lay still in the other bed. The doctor says their suffering is nearly over. Charls will make the coffins. Only little Sadie will live to see spring come. I hear her bubbly laugh with Carolina in the rocker. So young, so innocent. A midwife, Carolina came for the birthing. She will care for Sadie until my sister comes. Until the wild flowers fill the prairie once again.

Second Place Poetry by Susan Niemela Vollmer

Police Log Poem

*(According to the police log, on Wednesday night a mailbox was
smashed by a flying pumpkin.)*

I wish that I had looked up from my book and turned off the light
then stepped onto the back porch to watch the pumpkins
shake off their dinner-plate-sized leaves and prickly clinging vines
to levitate silently above the pumpkin patch
circle over the trees and head toward the bars on main street
where one of them would slurp down several pumpkin beers
before missing the curve on church hill and colliding with a
    mailbox
the rest of the crop would fly obliviously on their way
like a flock of orange geese rising toward the harvest moon

Second Place Creative Nonfiction by Marsha C. Porter

Laundry Stories: Beethoven

Roble Hall, Stanford University: Here to help my college student son in his recovery from a recent knee surgery, I balance an unwieldy armload of clothes and head for the laundry room. *A mother should not be in a college dorm.* I trail through narrow hallways, stifled in this California heat. *How hot is it, anyway?* A couple walks past me—students—arms twined 'round one another's waists. Her blue cloud skirt lofts on molten air, hair wisps languorous over her shoulders—humidity's sigh. His worn flip-flops snap bare heels. I snake the laundry room key from my pocket.

Moonlight Sonata, from a piano in the practice room next to the laundry room—repetition of single notes in musical phrase—*sostenuto*—up-up-up the scale, mirroring the day's heat, 94, 95, 96 degrees. *Legato*, one note at-a-time, one, two, and three, over-and-over . . . *How many times have I played that Adagio seduction, Moonlight Sonata?* I could set these clothes on the tiled floor, sit at the piano, find my way around the four sharps, the mid-mesmerization switch to five flats, stretch my fingers to that just-beyond-an-octave reach. *Moonlight Sonata* was not meant to be played in moonlight. It was meant to be played in heat—torrid, sultry, swoon of heat—in summer's late afternoon rush hour—traffic snarled, tangled, construction speed zones. Intermittent horns *presto fortissimo*, drivers' fingertips on steering wheels—*mezzo forte—taptaptaptap*, willing stalled traffic forward. Any Movement. At all. *The left hand, the right. How does this pied piper, Beethoven, create falling-through-the-stars delirium, from these simple notes?*

I unlock the laundry room door and, rebalancing the clothes in my arms, lean my back into it, pushing it open. Every washing machine is in use. Moist heat steams the windows. T-shirts snaggled on a large center table communicate identities: a faded orange: ULTIMATE FRISBEE CHAMPIONSHIP, a well-worn:

FREE TIBET! Another: SAY NO TO WAR WITH IRAQ.

I pull clean sogged clothes from a machine, lift the matted mess into a dryer, and push START. *No need for quarters for the machines?* Scooping heaps of miscellaneous clothes from the floor, I pile them onto the overloaded center table amidst tumbles of the unclaimed castaways.

I load my son's clothes and towels, and his roommate's pungent athletic shoes—tracked down by scent, to a spot underneath his desk—into the washing machine. Pilfering unidentifiable detergent from a nearby shelf, I start an overfilled wash load. I slip back through the door. The lock clicks, adamantly.

When I return to the laundry room, *Moonlight Sonata* is quiet. *Moonlight Sonata could last an entire wash cycle.* I take clothes from a dryer, folding them, leaving the underwear (female's) in a silky pile on top of the T-shirts and sweat pants. *Has anyone returned to this laundry room to find their dried clothes, folded? Would they stuff them into canvas bags, distractedly, while holding their place in* On the Genealogy of Morals—a text I find on top of the adjacent washer?

I push my son's clothes into the dryer, retrieving his roommate's wet shoes from the mix. I think about trying to make sense of the mess of clothes on the center table. *(Only a mother would have such an inclination.)* I can't tell what's dirty, what's clean. Too many errant socks. I give up.

Loading clothes in my arms, and untangling keys from my pocket, I head back to the dorm room. The same couple passes me, arms linking one another's waists, still—heat and humidity slowing their pace *legato . . . largo . . . give in to the heat; let it have its way; what else is there to do?* Sight obscured by the stack of clothes in my arms, I bump into a case of empty beer bottles, hearing the *clink* that only beer bottles in college dorms make. I sidestep a bag of garbage. Musical strains of Neal Young's "Heart of Gold," from an opened dorm room, wind through stairwells. *How can that be? Neal Young,* Harvest—*can still picture the album cover. What year is this? I have to get out of this dorm before my psyche gets sucked back into the '70s and I start wondering if my boyfriend, Brett, is in a stoned haze on this hot afternoon.*

Hot. I gather the gauze of my blue skirt in both hands, lifting the cloth from my bare legs. Catch some air. Any, at all. *Has to be 100 degrees.* I bunch the cloth of my skirt together in one hand, and with the other lift my hair—thick, languorous in the humidity—holding it off my neck, hoping for the slightest breeze against my skin. *I have serious studying to do for finals. I shouldn't be trying to do laundry right now. Will the library stay open late? Why are there never any machines that are not in use in this laundry room? What did I do with those quarters I need for the machines? I should look through that mess of clothes heaped on the laundry room table for Brett's T-shirt . . . the one I wore a few weeks ago. Which one was it, now?* I dig through the pile. A faded orange IMPEACH NIXON T-shirt, a well-worn HELL NO! WE WON'T GO! printed over a map of Viet Nam . . . a navy blue CARLETON COLLEGE hooded sweatshirt. *Wait a minute . . . is this it?* I shake out a wrinkled GRATEFUL DEAD T-shirt. I put my face in it, inhaling stale, burnt marijuana scent . . . . *This is definitely his shirt—the one Brett got when we were at that concert in St. Louis last summer.* I toss it onto my pile of clothes to be washed. *When can I get into the practice room? I have to work on that Beethoven sonata . . . the one that's driving me crazy with all the sharps and flats—those three notes over and over and over—that* Adagio sostenuto *repetition, tantalizing me, just past my reach, seducing me in ways I don't understand . . . .*

Second Place Fiction by Nicole Borg

South Side Spirits

The rain picked up suddenly, pounding the roof of the Intrepid like dozens of angry fists. Jordan turned the wipers to the highest setting. Even in town, visibility wasn't great. It would be worse on the highway.

Nervously, she turned onto the residential street that led to the bridge to Wisconsin. She didn't like driving in bad weather, and she wasn't looking forward to her visit with Aunt Sissy. Jordan hadn't talked to her since the divorce was finalized. Sissy would want to know the details, the precise unraveling of her seven-year marriage. Sissy was a fabulous knitter and would want the thread of the story start to finish, no stitch dropped, even if it was painful for Jordan.

Across the street, skeletal trees overgrew a faded sign, hand-painted, on the front of a tired old house. South Side Spirits and Grocery. Jordan blinked. She had never noticed the place before. On impulse, she turned at the corner. A Pabst sign hung over a side entrance.

She parked by the door but didn't turn the vehicle off. Even though it was Monday, the tiny gravel parking lot was empty. The place looked deserted, but Jordan could see a dim light coming through a small, hexagonal window.

The temptation to delay her trip was too strong. *One beer*, she thought and turned off the engine.

Jordan sprinted the few steps, hugging her coat to her. The screen door rattled as she pushed through it and opened the interior door. The bar was dead-empty, except for an old man bent over a table with a white bar rag in his hand. The smell of bleach was strong.

His eyes were blue and sharp, his face framed by unruly white tendrils, and his back hunched even as he straightened to meet her. He didn't smile, but assessed Jordan as if she were a mutt come in out of the rain. Jordan felt the heat rise in her cheeks, even as she shivered through wet clothes. She had been in bars like this before, where the clientele was the same each day. A new face wasn't always welcomed.

"Afternoon," Jordan said, brushing soggy hair out of her face.

The old man leaned against the patron's side of the bar. "Afternoon." His voice was as low and gravelly as Jordan had expected. The lighting was poor, but the man's face had a yellow cast. She wondered what illness he had and how far advanced it was.

"Were you hoping for something to drink?"

"A beer, actually," she said, waiting to be invited in, although that was ridiculous. It was a bar after all, not a private club. There was no bouncer at the door.

"You drink the dark stuff?" he asked, a little contemptuously.

"I'd drink whatever you had on tap."

His nod was almost imperceptible, but Jordan watched him cross to the back of the bar and knew this was as close to hospitality as she would get. She settled herself into a high-backed stool with a cracked, red vinyl seat. She laid her wet jacket across the seat next to her.

The old man didn't ask what she would have, but poured foaming beer from a spigot into an icy pint glass and set it on a white square of napkin in front of her.

Jordan smiled, as she raised the glass to her lips. "Thanks."

"Where you from?"

The beer was cold and smooth. She was glad she had stopped. "Austin."

"Family here?" The old man's blue eyes didn't look away from hers.

"I'm on my way to see my great aunt, up by Stockholm. She lives by herself. I try to get up there as often as I can."

"She don't have kids to look after her?"

"No. She was married once, but they never had kids."

"Me neither. My wife's been gone two years now in April. Didn't have no kids. Couldn't have 'em, so we acted like we hadn't wanted any."

Jordan nodded, not knowing what to say. The old man reached under the lip of the bar and pulled out a bowl of snack mix: pretzels and peanuts. "Thanks." She helped herself.

"You got a family of your own?"

Jordan chewed–the peanuts were salty, the pretzels a little stale. "I'm divorced." She said nothing of the miscarriages, her husband's affair, the failed marriage counseling. She would save all of that for Sissy. "As of last Wednesday."

"How's that for you?"

"I don't know yet. You're the first person I've told, aside from my mom and my sister."

"Fred," he said, extending his hand unexpectedly. She shook it firmly. Their eyes met and held. Her honesty had earned her something, but Jordan wasn't sure what.

"Jordan. Good to meet you."

"Marriage. Now that's work."

Jordan nodded. "More work than I would have ever guessed. I guess I should be thankful we didn't have any kids."

"You would have stayed with him?"

"No. I'd have left sooner. But at least I don't have to explain myself to a kid or anyone else."

"We all have to explain ourselves to someone." The old man turned and dusted the bottles of liquor carefully. "If not in this life, then in the next."

Jordan drank her beer in silence, taking in her surroundings. If there once was a grocery store, it was long gone. The place was a dive. The tourists would go to the bars on Main Street, with their high-top tables and expensive televisions. Here, the old bar was pitted, the little tables sported mismatched chairs, an ancient jukebox brooded in a dark corner and a small television with a crooked antennae sat behind the bar. A staircase in the back probably led to the old man's living quarters. It would always smell of stale beer up there. But the silence after everyone went home would be worse. It was the same silence that had settled over Jordan's house in the past week.

"How long were you married?"

"Forty-eight years. Always thought I'd go first. Hoped I would. Was the cancer that took her. Lung cancer. She didn't smoke. But owning the bar," he shrugged, "I s'pose it was the second-hand smoke. We didn't know anything about that back then."

"I'm sorry." Jordan's beer was almost gone and she wanted a second. *And a third and a fourth.* She found herself thinking of Eric and how he wasn't coming back, not ever.

"Lung cancer is ugly. Hacking-up blood and wheezing all the time. Doctors sent her home to die. Nothing they could do. So it was me and her, and the nurses coming twice a day. It got so I thought I'd go crazy just listening to her breathe."

"I would have gotten drunk." Jordan nodded toward the neat rows of bottles.

"Did that once. But then I couldn't take care of her. Woke up dizzy and heard her crying. Most ashamed I've ever been."

Jordan swirled the dregs of her beer in the glass. It was time to go. The rain had let up some, and Stockholm wasn't that far. Aunt Sissy would have made dinner.

Fred said something she didn't catch.

"What's that?"

Jordan studied the old man's stooped reflection in the bar mirror. She thought there were tears in his eyes, but she couldn't be sure. "Made up for it though."

"For getting drunk?"

"I ended it."

Jordan thought for a moment that she had misunderstood.

Fred went on, "I didn't hurt her. I just couldn't watch no more. Hell, it wasn't going to get better."

Jordan was suddenly cold; her wet jeans clung to her uncomfortably and strands of damp hair stuck to her face. "How?"

Fred blinked hard and met her eyes. "Doesn't matter. We all have to answer to someone. I answer to her first, then to Him."

Jordan didn't move. A silence lengthened between them, softened by the falling rain.

"Looks like you're done with that beer," he said, pointing to her empty glass.

"Yes." Jordan fumbled for her purse.

Fred held up a hand.

"No, that's nice of you. I'll pay."

"Can't let you do that. I'm not open."

Jordan looked up.

"Raining so hard, you must not have seen the "Closed" sign. I close sometimes on Mondays. A rainy Monday tends to be slow. Nope, I can't take your money. We're just two people enjoying each other's company."

Jordan got unsteadily to her feet, feeling as if she'd drunk ten beers. "Thanks," she managed, but Fred had gone back to his cleaning.

Jordan left without putting on her coat. She started the Intrepid and cranked the heat, and sat with her hands on the wheel. The car filled with the voice of the slow rain, a confession so loud she couldn't hear herself crying.

Poetry by Sister Kate Martin

Edge

I understand an edge: a border, isn't it, a first wedge into something else, something new? Somewhere you can only get past by falling, falling and giving yourself into the hands of gravity, flying to the next you, the one that only appears beyond the limits of what came before. There are sharp edges that cut your fingers when you cling to them, and there are long concavities that curl upwards and lift you till you are flung into space, a free place wide enough for fear, euphoria and second thoughts, a space where something is born that turns you wide-eyed toward the welcoming curve of newness, and you find yourself at the beginning, the threshold, the other side.

Poetry by Jan Chronister

Sweet Tooth

Milk glass dish
glimmered like a chalice
luring the faithful.
I could lift its lid noiselessly,
praying for kitchen conversation
to mask my intentions.

Manna gleamed inside—
Brach's Pick-a-Mix
supplanted by candy corn and
jelly beans in season.

Mother religiously stocked the dish.
One summer my tooth decay
reached a record fourteen fillings.

In high school
I applied my craft
to removing screens,
sneaking out for stronger sweets.

In college I crept home late,
sated with desserts.
Betrayed by locked doors,
I waited until dawn glazed
Milwaukee
and Daddy left for work.

I packed up and moved out,
taking my sweet tooth with me.

Fiction by Sandra Clough

Paris Morning

Carefully balancing her espresso and croissant, Margaux headed toward a small café table that caught the morning sun. She smiled as she settled, intoxicated by the smoky aroma of French roast wafting up from the tiny cup.

The throaty voice of Edith Piaf floated through an open window. The sound was scratchy and distorted, but it made Margaux wish she could have visited Paris during the '30s. From what she'd read, the city had a gaiety back then that was lost forever when the war started.

Even so, it was still a magical place.

Margaux glanced around the empty courtyard. She hoped nearby seats would be claimed by Parisians, rather than chattering American tourists. French voices always seemed to be filled with music and romance and, even though she hadn't yet mastered the language, she was content to let the words wash over her, enjoying their beauty—like when she went to the opera at home.

As she relaxed into the warm, luxuriant sunshine, Margaux closed her eyes and pictured Pierre rounding the corner with his blinding smile and a passionate kiss. She wished he would hurry. When they were apart, she began to fear he was a figment of her imagination.

After a moment, Margaux opened her eyes. Still alone, she picked up the flaky croissant. Pierre wouldn't mind that she hadn't waited. The buttery pastry dissolved in her mouth.

Nothing in the world—not Italian bread, nor English scones, nor Greek Baklava—could match this delicacy invented by the French.

She sipped her espresso, savoring the pungent richness. Why had it taken so long to come back here? This break from her hectic life at home made her feel like a new person.

Suddenly, her reverie was interrupted. Somewhere in the distance, a bell sounded. It might have been a church bell, perhaps being rung from the spire of a cathedral that was hundreds of years old, or maybe it was the clang of a French ambulance careening down one of the narrow, cobblestone streets that ran along the Seine. It was so faint, Margaux couldn't be sure.

She heard it again, but this time it was louder. *Ding-dong. Ding-dong.*

Inside the building behind her, a door slammed. She heard footsteps and excited voices drawing nearer. The grainy squeal of a sliding glass door being pushed open made her jump.

Margaux shook her head, trying to get her bearings.

"Mom, why are you sitting out here? It's almost ten! You said you'd take us to soccer. Remember?"

Margaret sighed. "Calm down, honey," she said. "We've got plenty of time."

Picking up her dishes and carrying them inside to the kitchen, Margaret smiled. Tomorrow she'd grind some Italian roast and make a cappuccino. It was time Margherita made another trip to Italy.

Poetry by Charmaine Pappas Donovan

Heavenly Bodies

We were not cheap tricks as we walked the streets.
While our bodies bloomed in matching flowered shirts,
we poured ourselves into rear-hugging stovepipe pants.
The rubber toes of our new bumper tennies
shined like childhood patent leather.

We were hipless, girlfriends
halfway through our teens,
our dolls ditched for real action.
Dark-haired Barbies, on the lookout
for their faceless, groovy Kens.

We walked the sidewalks
while sun and moon beams
tracked our aimless route.
We thought we knew
what to do with ourselves,
where to find out.

We traipsed through downtown,
wore our youth like tiaras
on the glistening hair of beauty queens.
Main Street was our runway.
Our thoughts circled like our walks,
as familiar and repetitive as the lyrics
to every favorite Beatles' song.

Up and down alleys,
hitchhiking highways,
we carried our dreams on our backs
like magic carpets.
They warmed us on cold nights
when coats were thin
and no one seemed to notice
how we twinkled,
how this orbit was meant
to steer us from that lukewarm town
toward a life we could grasp
as well as the galaxy;
a place whose gravity
held our bodies earthbound,
kept us from melting the stars.

Honorable Mention Fiction by Niomi Rohn Phillips

Dawn

Julie intended to marry a forceful and decisive man, someone with goals, someone as unlike her father as possible. She wanted security and stability in her life. She met Stan on a blind date her sophomore year in college.

"I've had it with blind dates," she'd told her roommate Joyce. "The last guy you lined me up with was a 6' tall nerd. I felt like I was in a vice on the dance floor, and I got a crick in my neck trying to look up and carry on a conversation."

"Please. . . A big favor," Joyce begged. "My date's friend loves to dance. He's a senior and a 4.0," she added for enticement.

He was clean-cut, good-looking. Blue eyes, blonde crew cut, four inches taller than Julie. Lean and muscular. And a great dancer. Following his "Rock Around the Clock" was effortless: strong hold on her elbow, the hint of a push in the direction he wanted to move, firm grasp on her hand on the return twirl. He held her close for "String of Pearls," but didn't press against her so she'd have to worry about what he expected later in the back seat of the car.

After the dance, he suggested they take a walk along the river. "I'll be leaving right after graduation," he told her. "Jobs are really good for geologists in the oil industry, so I'm going to the U. of Wisconsin for a master's degree."

His breath was sweet and the kiss gentle. She learned later that he was obsessive about personal hygiene and sex was always gentle.

They got married—in Stan's church—after his graduation in June and left for Madison. He enrolled in graduate school, they moved into married student housing, and she got a job in the university registrar's office.

Two years later, Texaco sent Stan to Colorado with his Master's Degree in hand. They bought a starter house in the suburbs, a neighborhood of young couples with two or three kids. Rick was born on schedule a year later; then Susan—a two year age difference, all according to Stan's master plan.

The neighborhood men went off to work every morning; women stayed home. Laundry on Mondays, vacuum on Fridays, bridge on Wednesday nights, neighborhood barbecues on the weekends.

About the time Julie was getting bored with that scene and her role, Frances Cole moved into the neighborhood. She was a sassy sparkplug with the audacity to join the male huddle around the barbecue grill Friday nights. Not popular with the men. They used words like "mouthy" and "overbearing." She made the women uneasy. Dropped her kids off at daycare every morning and went to an office. She made Julie restless. They became best friends.

Stan said Frances' husband was pussy-whipped. "You can see her every day if you want, but don't bring her women's lib ideas into this house."

Stan was transferred to Oklahoma. Part of his plan. Transfer meant promotion. They bought a bigger house in a better neighborhood with the same follow-your-man kind of women, now lounging around swimming pools. Julie yearned for a Frances Cole.

She didn't have the guts to break away from all of it, buck the system. Besides, what could she do without a college degree? She made timid efforts to change her life—joined a consciousness-raising group and started looking for a job.

"If a hobby job will keep you out of the doldrums, go ahead; just make sure you have time to entertain when the brass comes to town," Stan said.

Job interviews were humiliating. "What job experience do you have? What is your educational background? Do you have references?" *I quit college and worked so my husband could go. My degree is a PHT—putting hubby through. I don't have any references because my work experience was five moves and two decades ago.* She finally got hired in the registrar's office at the local college.

Fall semester, Professor Tom Ferraro, new to the faculty, missed the deadline for submitting grades for his Intro to Psychology class. The Registrar directed him to Julie.

"I've really goofed up here," he said, even his brown eyes smiling, as he sat down next to her desk. "I hate all this paperwork. I'm terrible at it. I'd really be grateful for your help."

The humility unnerved her. Most faculty expected clerical staff to kiss their ass. He sat beside her desk several times during the next days, checking the grade sheets for two-hundred students. They leaned close. He brushed his hair away from his face in a boyish way. They spoke softly so as not to disturb the room full of other clerks. It felt intimate to Julie. Their hands touched passing papers. Her skin prickled. She shivered inside.

On impulse, she walked across campus to his office one afternoon to give him copies of the final worksheets. She knocked. He smiled when he opened the door. Piles of papers, books, and notebooks were stacked on the floor, lining the walls in front of floor-to-ceiling overflowing book shelves. "Stay a minute," he motioned to a sagging ancient easy chair. She did. She went back the next day. Then she took her lunch break there every day. They locked the door.

In bed with Stan at home, she faked and prayed he wouldn't know the difference. Tom hovered in the background. She wanted to say his name. She forced herself not to talk about him. She fantasized about a life with him. He'd never shown any interest in her teenage kids, but. . . .

Her secret made rebellion at home easier. She not only simmered inside but argued with Stan about everything from Susan's curfew to campus Vietnam War protests.

"What the hell's wrong with you?" he asked.

She wasn't prepared for the transfer to Beaumont, Texas. "The big promotion," Stan announced. "Our last move. The climate's great! You're gonna love it!"

She reminded herself that he was "the major bread winner." She had a menial job and no education. How could she support herself? How could she manage alone? What about the kids?

The car drove itself to the campus and Tom's office. When she told him, he said, "I'll miss you."

Beaumont did turn out to be the last stop. "You don't need to get a job," Stan said. "The little money you earn just goes to taxes. We have to join the Country Club now that I'm in the corporate office. You can play your bridge there and get to know the wives."

She had a big house to decorate and furnish. There was no point in looking for a job anyway until they were settled. She joined the bridge group. She chauffeured Rick to football practice and games. Found a comrade at Susan's soccer games.

"There's an hour between these damn games," Karen complained at a tournament. "Let's find a lounge and have a glass of wine." That became a pleasant habit.

A decade slipped by. Susan and Rick left home.

Julie played daytime bridge now, twice a week with lunch and martinis. The rosy glow lasted to dinner wine. She shopped at the Galleria in Houston with her friends. She tucked the Ferraro interlude away to savor—one brief affair, one flash of daring in her secure life.

Friday nights she met Stan at the club for cocktails and the dinner dance. They'd been dancing forever—moved like one person on the dance floor. "You're good," Stan whispered, aware of people watching them.

Some days she even liked Stan—some days, some not. Sex usually resolved the latest contention. They were Fifties people. They took "till death do us part" seriously.

The wind was blowing as Stan loaded his hunting paraphernalia into the SUV. He and his buddies were driving to a hunting lodge in the hill country. *More than 3200 acres, hunters guaranteed to get trophy deer.* Barbaric, Julie thought. Worse than shooting from a deer stand in the Wisconsin woods. Her dad was never interested in hunting.

Stan coughed and spit in the driveway. "You've been hacking for days," she fumed. "Why can't you give up this stupid ritual? You're sick. What is so sacred about being there for the opening day hunt?"

He ignored her. She didn't say good luck or goodbye. *He's bullheaded.* For the hundredth time, she resigned herself to it. Things would never change.

His hunting buddies called from a hospital in Junction late afternoon opening day. The life she'd known was over. She would have to force herself to get out of bed every morning now and figure out who she was. The woman she'd become was mostly reflection, and her mirror was gone.

Poetry by Pat Spilseth

Pain Has Strong Arms

Strong as the passions that rocked my body
when you held me in your arms,
your detachment causes pain,
loss, abandonment.

You couldn't know.
Women are never what we seem to be . . .
always there is the girl you see
as well as the woman hidden inside.

Too wise to tell you all my thoughts.
Certainly I'll not share feelings you'd reject.
My intuition knows
no man wants
to know
everything
about his woman.

I didn't become the woman you know
overnight.
I've been in the making
for a lifetime.
So many doors to open.
Some need to be closed.

I aim to be the heroine
of my own story.
It's sad to grow old,
but oh so nice to ripen . . . .

My most profound relationship
is the one with myself.

Creative Nonfiction by Sharon Harris

Rudderless

That is how I will feel when Mother is gone.

Sometimes I envy people who have lived in lots of places and don't have many belongings. I have often thought that older people who have lived in many different places must have a much easier time of it when they must move to Assisted Living or even the Nursing Home. They have become okay with saying goodbye to things and places. They are okay with change.

And then there is me. I have lived in virtually the same place my whole life. When I work somewhere, I work there for twenty plus years. I have an amazing stick-to-it-ivness. I hate change. I love stability and routine. I love to preserve things. I keep memories alive. I am the caretaker, the preserver, the keeper and protector of things.

Mother and Dad, the farm, the farmhouse, the old barn. These things were my childhood. They are my childhood. They are important, my anchor. The outside world was chaotic and messy and unpredictable. The farm was unchanging. You had no choice but to be there for chores; the animals depended on you. My folks were steady and solid. We lived in one spot and one spot only. There was no divorce, no upheaval.

Later on, when I got out into life, I was startled to realize that not everyone had a rock-steady childhood. I was always successful in school and learning came easily to me. Work came easily too and I rose to the top as a supervisor. It was a while before I realized that not everyone had such stability to start them out in life. I had solid ground beneath my feet the whole time and my folks were steady support. Other kids were moved from place to place; step-parents moved in and out of their lives; sometimes there was abuse or cruelty. For me, success was easy; for other kids, success was just getting through the day. It took a long time for me to quit being so critical of others who were not successful.

So, here I am. Fifty-eight. Losing Dad was very hard. But as long as Mother is still here and still living on the old homestead, well—it seems like things are still kind of okay. My childhood is still there, preserved in the old barn, the old farmhouse, and Mother.

So, this solid beginning, this constancy of my parents and my good childhood, this is all still in place. When Mother is gone, then it will feel like the whole world has shifted. I will feel lost in uncharted waters, rudderless.

*Note: This is an editorial board member as well as a member of the board of directors of the Jackpine Writers' Bloc. This work, and all work in the book by the editorial board members or board of directors of the JWB, is not eligible to go to the celebrity judges or receive prizes.

Poetry by Tarah L. Wolff

Reliability

Painting of a little girl
leaning against a face
as tall as she is,
the face of a giant
black work horse.

The gentleness of that little kiss,
and the reliability of that huge face,
hangs on the wall
down the hall
from her room.

Every day at breakfast,
there and back again,
she shuffles by the painting
that could have been of her,
ninety years ago.

Now she leans on steel
and there is no risk that
it may step back
and let her fall,
no risk at all.

*Note: This is an editorial board member of the Jackpine Writers' Bloc. This work, and all work in the book by the editorial board members or board of directors of the JWB, is not eligible to go to the celebrity judges or receive prizes.

Poetry by Doris Bergstrom

I Don't Want to Know

Don't tell me how night captures dew.
I want to hold the magic—
pretend invisible hands scatter droplets
while I dream.

If the maple tree doesn't drip
its sap to sweeten spring
and pussy willows don't puff their fur
for us to pet, don't let me know.

If the owl isn't hooting me awake
and fireflies aren't flashing for me
to come outside, don't tell me.
I won't believe you.

And if the great blue heron doesn't dip
its silver wings just to squawk the river
and all of us awake,
Please don't let me know it isn't so.

And I won't tell you either.

Poetry by Adrian S. Potter

The Intervention Soliloquy

Your doubts hang heavy and low
like winter coats on wire hangers.

The night has ceased
to tempt you with reasons to smile
and discretion is a grenade
you've tossed through every broken window
of what's been forsaken, so you seek refuge
in the condemned building inside you: the rotted
beams overhead, the warped staircases,
the rickety scaffold;

according to the excuses tattooed on your tongue
you have no plans, no backup,
or backup plans: all memory feels fictional,

the future meaningless

now that your spirit is
lukewarm like red wine
spilled down a sink drain,

now that everything is upsetting
like brown liquor on an empty stomach.

Your downfall didn't happen
overnight. Or perhaps it did:

your serrated silence, the crooked little secrets;
your bittersweet narcissism, the rebellious archetypes.

You've become apprenticed to the frenzied environment.

Will these words meander off their intended path
like hikers using an outdated map?

Will the moon continue being so full of itself
that it cannot see past its own light, through its celestial facade?

You should bury more than the past.
You should subtract the minor losses.
You should change.

Creative Nonfiction by Mike Lein

Movin' On Up

You won't hear much open talk about it, but a social class system exists up here in the North Country that rivals those of medieval times. Like it or not, people fall into four distinct categories that they likely will never escape.

First there's the ordinary "tourist"—the lowest on the class totem pole. Tourists show up for a weekend or a week and then disappear—sometimes forever. One step up are the "summer people," those who own lake homes and have the means to spend the summer "Up North" before fleeing south to warmer climates by Labor Day. I fit into the third class—the "wannabes." We spend weekends and a few weeks at our cabins, four seasons of the year, always hoping to move up to the highest social class—the "locals."

The locals are a hardy bunch, making a living at everything from farming to banking. Locals come in many shapes, sizes, and nationalities but they are all universally good at one thing. They can spot one of us lower class people a mile away. Sometimes they even figure out how to make a buck off us—something that has so far escaped me.

The tourists have the hardest time fitting in. Most are easy to spot with their pale skin and clashing shorts and T-shirts, wandering aimlessly around town clutching shopping lists. Usually their list includes sunscreen, bug repellant, beer, shiny fishing tackle, and that forgotten swimsuit. A boat or camper hitched to a fancy SUV plastered with "Wall Drug" bumper stickers is another dead giveaway.

The summer people have an equally hard time blending in since they hang around and repeatedly use the services offered by locals. The stereotypical summer person is older than most tourists, much better dressed, and prefers to drive an upscale four door sedan. An older well-known male summer person may be referred to as "that rich guy from the cities" by locals. This is not necessarily a derogatory term. However, the word "guy" can be substituted with a less complimentary term if the person is thought to be arrogant and/or tight with his money.

A notable subset of the summer people deserves mention—the "summer girl." Lest you doubt this is a defined term, ask any male local who is or once was a teenager. He will gladly point out nearby examples. These might vary due to personal preference but will likely be well-tanned, well-dressed, attractive young females. Summer girls are a universal fantasy of young male locals. They appear for the warm sunny summer, flash their smiles and good looks around town, and then mysteriously disappear. There may also be "summer boys" that keep the young female locals guessing.

That brings us to my "wannabe" situation. I was a local once, for a while, many years ago. I worked for Jack the cement guy, played pool at the Legion on Thursday nights against the old guy in the Hawaiian shirt, and helped out at the gas station when Bill needed a break. I could spot tourists, summer people, and especially summer girls, with the best of the locals. Sadly, I had to move south many years ago. For much too long, I was just another tourist. Thank God, I was able to break free from that sorry state when I built my cabin.

It's unlikely that I will ever be mistaken for a summer person, especially a rich guy from the cities, due to my budget, humble cabin, and lack of style. I do occasionally kid myself that someday I will fit back in with locals. This fantasy is always burst, just like those old weak attempts at flirting with summer girls.

I pulled into the boat repair shop on a Sunday afternoon with a sick boat. It never occurred to me that brother-in-law Darv and I wouldn't blend in. We had on our work clothes, stinky and trashed from a weekend of cabin projects and fishing. The boat wasn't a flashy decked-out ski boat or a glittering bass boat. It was a classic 14-foot red Lund, pulled by my well-used truck. Even so, we never stood a chance. The mechanic listened to the problem description, offered a diagnosis, and quoted a very reasonable price.

"Great," I said. "When will you get to it?"

Without hesitation he replied, "I'll make sure it's ready when you come back up for Memorial Day." Clearly I wasn't a summer person or a rich guy from the cities. And I wasn't a local who would need the boat ASAP. At least he didn't mistake me for a lowly tourist.

I'm not sure how many years it will take to become a local once we retire to the cabin. Blending in will probably mean spending time hanging out at the coffee shop, helping with church functions, joining the VFW, and maybe working part-time, helping some business separate money from the tourists and summer people. Sometimes I do have hope.

The other day I was wandering the aisles of the hardware store when a tourist stopped me. It was obvious he was not from around here. He had the whole sunburn, shorts, sandals, T-shirt, glazed-eye-thing going. "Say," he asked. "Where can I get a propane tank filled around here?"

I didn't have to think. "Head west about five blocks to the stoplight. The gas station on the northwest corner has a bulk tank and fills 'em cheap."

"Thanks!" He walked away happy, obviously pleased with himself, satisfied that he had tapped into local knowledge.

I know it wasn't much of a challenge, helping out a hapless tourist. But I was gloating a bit as I plopped my mousetraps and birdseed down on the checkout counter and struck up a conversation with the local gal behind it. "Seems pretty busy in here today."

"Yeah," she replied. "There's lots of you 'cabin people' up here this weekend."

Note: This is an editorial board member of the Jackpine Writers' Bloc. This work, and all work in the book by the editorial board members or board of directors of the JWB, is not eligible to go to the celebrity judges or receive prizes.

Poetry by Tim J. Brennan

Ducks Tell no Tales

I watch from my kitchen
window as five mallards stride,
web-footed to my neighbor's feeder
Yesterday there were six;
last week, seven
I walk outside to confront them
and from a distance
crouch to their level
I exhort them to tell me, please,
what's been happening
to their numbers?
Five silent mallards glare back,
blue eyes reveal nothing
but their nature
As I return home, I wonder:
are we divided by the silence
or by a world?

Poetry by Laura L. Hansen

Driftwood

They gutter ashore,
sloughed off
by the river.

They lie
on the muddy banks
for days, weeks, more
until we come along
and pick them up,
admiring their sun-
bleached flanks, their
deeply articulated pores.

Driftwood as weathered
as old bones.

This one is shaped
like a small rhino's horn,
disparate from the body
that once held it, smooth
as a sheathed sword.

And this one has
a slender leg rising up
to a gnarled hip bone, a
partial pelvis.

And in my hand, a
hollowed-out burl, so like
an orbital socket, missing
only the knowing eye.

From this collection alone,
we can imagine ourselves
building a small animal
piece by grey-wood piece,
giving it life, becoming
gods.

Poetry by Scott Stewart

In their sorrow

shrouded in soiled rags,
they are
trammeled in anguished herding—
loaded for passage:
a side-depot replacing Scheol
in an Auschwitz gloaming.

In their sorrow, they are
violated
shadows defecating latent
vestiges of hope.
Teshuvas invoked within echoed lowings
of deliverance,

denied.
In their sorrow
borne by creviced limbs, shriveled chests,

and sunken bellies,
they wear their mantle deep
into the stink of burnt flesh.

In their sorrow
gasping,

beseeching
the smoking fetor
to baptize shriven souls . . .
evaporating the ink from the ashes
of emptied cattle stalls.

Note: This is an editorial board member as well as a member of the board of directors of the Jackpine Writers' Bloc. This work, and all work in the book by the editorial board members or board of directors of the JWB, is not eligible to go to the celebrity judges or receive prizes.

Honorable Mention Fiction by Lindsy J. O'Brien

Ghost on the Bus

I shouldn't have lied when Stella asked me if I could see her sister's ghost.

I wasn't even sure that was what she was asking, at first, because she didn't say it out loud. Stella stopped talking when Ava died, just quit using her voice altogether. She was a third grader and old enough to know she was supposed to answer back when an adult talked to her, so I was a little annoyed that she didn't get in trouble.

"The poor little thing," my mom said when I told her. "Just give her time, Ky. She'll come around."

Two weeks after the funeral, when Stella slid silently into the mud-brown bus seat beside me, I was surprised. I made room for her automatically. No one paid attention or seemed to think it strange to see a nine-year-old girl sit down next to a fifth grade boy. Of course, they were used to seeing Ava and me together.

Stella was small and weedy with knobbed knees and ankles. She looked nothing like Ava.

That's not entirely true. Maybe they look the same a little, through the eyes, the way they both lifted their straw-colored eyebrows when they smiled.

Ava had green eyes, though, green as grass. Stella's weren't green, but next to her on the bus, I realized that I didn't actually know what color they were. I glanced at her in the seat beside me, behind the wisps of strawberry blond hair that escaped her headband. Gray, I decided. Maybe gray-blue. The color of a storm cloud. I missed Ava's eyes, the way they sparkled like green ocean waves.

Stella's eyes were dull, and her pale face was a statue-face. She didn't have freckles like Ava did.

"What's up?" I asked, not expecting an answer. Under her winter jacket, she had on a blue striped T-shirt that had once belonged to Ava. I remembered how Ava wore that shirt two summers ago when my mom drove us down to Duluth, to the beach along Lake Superior. We were playing tic-tac-toe with magic markers in the backseat of my mom's car (Mom didn't worry over stuff like magic marker spots on car seats), and Ava's red marker slipped and added a blood-red line that crossed the stripes on her shirt.

"Mom'll kill me!" she said, spitting on her thumb and rubbing at the stain like I'd seen her mother do sixty-five-thousand times.

Yup. There it was on Stella's shirt, a faded crimson smear on her stomach, just below her ribcage.

Stella looked past me with her not-quite-Ava eyes.

"So, you still aren't talking then?" I rearranged my backpack on my lap so the corner of my math book didn't stab into my leg.

Stella shook her head.

I think she'd gotten skinnier since the funeral. Her jeans sagged over her thighs and around her middle so that she had to winch them up with a belt to keep them from falling off. The jeans were probably Ava hand-me-downs, too. It made me wonder if there might be little bits of Ava trapped in the fabric. Maybe that's why Stella was wearing them.

I gave up trying to talk to her, instead stared out the bus window at the crispy-dried-up November morning. The sun was a peeking eyeball behind a hill of overburden, which was the word we learned in school for the stuff left over after the mines took the iron ore out of the dirt we lived on. All our hills were fake like that, flat-topped and hiding under a wig of scrabbly trees and bushes. I didn't like the overburden. I wanted to live in a place where the hills were hills, or maybe mountains. It bothered me when things were different from what they were supposed to be.

Stella moved beside me. Out of the corner of my eye, I saw her unzip her backpack and pull out a notebook and a blue crayon. Stella always used crayons instead of pencils to write even though Ava told her not to.

"I can't read your writing as it is, Stell," she complained.

Stella flipped the notebook open and began to write, if you could call that mess of blue lines and scratches writing. Ava's letters had been neat, perfect. Better sometimes than our fifth grade teacher's. My own writing looked more like Stella's and usually had more spelling mistakes.

After a minute or so, Stella tore the sheet of paper from her notebook, folded it into a messy rectangle, and held it out to me.

"Is that for me?" I asked needlessly. It felt too strange to sit in silence, like we were in our own little church in the middle of the laughter and shouts of the kids around us. Stella nodded. Her headband slipped on her head so a few more strands of hair burst free and reached with static-cling for the seat behind her.

I unfolded the paper and spread it against my backpack. A few shreds of spiral notebook edging fell onto the sticky black floor.

"I can see Ava. Can you?"

That's all the note said. I didn't lift my eyes from it right away, trying to make it mean something other than what I thought it meant. Stella's white finger poked into my line of sight, tapping the last two words. I looked up at her.

"You can see Ava? I don't understand."

Stella knit her eyebrows and snatched the note back. She held it to her notebook and wrote another line below the first in the same waxy blue penmanship. This time, she held it up for me to see.

"Ava talks to me. I can hear her. She says that you can, too."

I swallowed. It was easy to picture Ava next to me in this seat that we'd shared every school day since kindergarten.

"Howdy, Ky-boy." That's how she greeted me, a joke she thought was hilarious. She'd even tip a pretend cowboy hat at me if she was in a good mood. In some ways, the imaginary Ava was more real to me than the real-life Stella who sat in her place.

But I couldn't *actually* see her. I couldn't *actually* hear her.

"Is she here, right now?" I asked slowly.

Stella bobbed her head at me. Then she raised her hand again and pointed to the page.

"Can you?"

She tapped her fingertip to the question three times, three even paper-crinkling beats. Then she looked up at me.

"I don't know," I said. It was like someone flipped a switch behind Stella's eyes then. The tiny bit of hope that had flared up behind them was doused like a campfire in the rain. Her hands holding the notebook paper dropped, but her finger remained rooted to the question.

"Can you?"

No. I couldn't see Ava right now, right here, just as if she had never left.

But it wasn't like I didn't see her at all. The dent in the seat in front of Stella . . . that was from Ava's knees, from when she propped them up to rest a book on her legs all those hundreds of days on this same bus, in this same seat. I saw her sandy hair spilled over her shoulders, thick like a horse tail, and the twelve freckles that fell across her cheeks and nose like early stars.

I heard her voice, too. "Howdy, Ky-boy!" Her laugh that started in her belly like a toddler's and bubbled up so that I couldn't not laugh along with her.

So maybe it wasn't a lie, the answer I gave her little sister.

"Stella? I can see her, too."

Poetry by Connie Claire Szarke

Paris 1954

Lucie is six, bouncing a ball forth and back
with her playmates until it is time for them to
go inside and sit quietly in rows on little
wooden chairs like the big ones in church.
They listen to *Soeur Marie*, who tells them
stories about the Bible figures, which she
manipulates on a felt board. Afterward, Sister
hands out holy cards to the children. Lucie's
card is a picture of a saint with the same name
as her own. "How many of you girls would
like to become Sisters? Raise your hands
high," sings *Soeur Marie*. Each child looks
determinedly at the others in an effort to raise
her hand the very highest of all. "Jesus died
for your sins. Did you know that, children?"
"*Oui, ma Soeur*," chant the little girls in
unison. "Repeat after me," orders *Soeur Marie*:
"I AM SIN." "I AM SIN," cry the little girls,
one louder than the rest. "Very good,
children." And *Soeur Marie* claps her hands
three times.

Poetry by Cheryl Weibye Wilke

Family Farms

A full cup of faint stars
pulsed through the mist

blanketing nameless farms quiet
as sodden fields in the dark.

Dark except for the dying
embers of their solitary

yard lights glowing
milk-glass blue. Such sad

and beautiful faces.
Sad because they are so lost.

Beautiful because once
they were young and close

as sisters in a constellation.
Girls with dust in their hair

and dew on their toes dancing
before harvest moons—

ripe and full wishing
upon a falling star

that they might set out
for a city-light world.

　　　Sad because

the roots of their hearts
never left the rain.

Poetry by Bob Bjelkengren

War

The four stars pin maps
with red, white, and blue markers.
The suits smoke cigars

far from the front lines.
In air conditioned comfort,
they play their "chess game."

The pawns' pressed fatigues
are wrinkled in body bags
for the long flight home.

Poetry by Marge Barrett

Shot Down: Number One

i.

Mr. Van Uden,
you shot our mutt dog, but Luck
lived on, three-legged.

ii.

You chased us—*Mongrels*!
but we bombed your giant hill,
our sleds, slick weapons.

iii.

Old Man Van Uden,
our nemesis, you stirred us
with frightful delight.

Fiction by Cindy Fox

Let the Fireworks Begin

Brother John, on all fours beside my gas grill, is trying to read the food-splattered instructions to start my barbecue. Scraping at the encrusted grease with his thumbnail, he grumbles to himself, "I can read something now . . . 'Turn on gas control knob. Engage the igniter switch several times' . . . but I did that already."

I stick my head around the screen door. "John, did you remember to open the valve on the propane tank?"

"Sure," he lies as he reaches through the cobwebs for the valve. "Guess I didn't open it all the way." The propane gas hisses like a mean old cat. Sensing danger, the dogs nervously back off.

Lurching to his feet, John fumbles in his pockets. "Hey, does anyone have some matches?"

The men on the deck don't hear him. They are in a heated discussion, no doubt sparked by too many beers.

"Oh, forget it. I don't need 'em."

John flicks in his lit cigarette. The flame's hungry tongue lashes out at him, drawing screeches of alarm from the men now standing at attention. John dodges back like a boxer avoiding a fast uppercut punch .

Brother Mike, wearing a cap depicting NOTHING RUNS LIKE A DEERE, came over for one beer two hours ago. He has cut hay on the field waiting to be baled—a task guaranteed to fall on the Fourth of July. Mike laughs boisterously from a lawn chair that he has tipped back at a dangerous angle. "Hey John," he roars, his red face flushed from working in the sun, "I thought we were going to wait until it was dark to start the fireworks!"

"Got 'er done," John haughtily mimics Larry, the Cable Guy. He draws a hefty swig off his Old Mil and hollers, "Becky, did you boil those brats in beer like I told you to?"

"Hold your horses. I'll bring 'em out in a minute."

A van pulls onto the front lawn of my cabin, parking dangerously close to the river. Abandoning their game of bocce ball, the kids scream with delight, "Uncle Rick is here! Uncle Rick is here!"

My brother Rick, a big man with broad shoulders, wearily slides out of the truck. He has just returned from South Dakota with supplies. The kids hover around him like pesky flies as he unloads boxes of fireworks—none of them legal in the State of Minnesota.

My sister Doreen and her family arrive late. Arms wrapped around a super-sized bowl of potato salad, Doreen hurries up the driveway. The dogs rush up to her, and she screams, "Will someone get these dogs outta here?"

Doreen's daughter, Megan, senses the dire consequences should Mom stumble while carrying in the potato salad. It's a known fact: farm dogs prefer table scraps over store-bought dog food. With a fallen willow branch, Megan switches at the leaping dogs, ensuring Mom's safe passage to the cabin door.

Inside the cabin, the kitchen counters are covered with crock pots, platters, and bowls of food. Each dish is rich and oozing with calories that Dr. Oz would warn us will lead to an early death.

The women laugh and chatter, sharing recipes on their hot dishes, salads, and desserts. The men circle the food, sampling appetizers, and make guesses on what NFL team Brett Favre will play on this year. The rambunctious kids run in and out of the cabin, letting in a slew of flies that make a beeline to the food.

My son Pete's girlfriend, Melanie, offers me a glass of her tart lemonade punch. I sense vodka may be the ingredient with the punch as I detect a slight slur in her speech.

"No thanks, Mel. I'll grab a cold soda instead. I need to keep my head on straight until dinner is served."

Looking out the screen door, I worry my cabin will start on fire. John stands over the blaze, waving away the billowing smoke.

I rush to his side. "John, what are you doing? You're ruining the meat!"

"I'm just sealing in the meat's juices by grilling them on high heat first. I know what I'm doing. Don't worry about it. You always worry too much."

Like bodies pulled from a burning building, the hamburgers and brats are rescued from the flames. The burgers clink on the plate like hockey pucks. The brats, their casings ruptured and charred, roll off to lie next to their defeated companions.

After dinner, we settle around the bonfire, waiting for the fireworks to begin. Rick sets up the rocket launcher, and lectures the youngsters to stay by their parents. As the sun finally sinks into the shimmering river, the countdown begins. Rick starts igniting fireworks, each surpassing the last one. The family hoots and hollers and Rick, grinning, is elated that he's in charge of this razzle-dazzle display.

A time-out is called. Darkness also brings Minnesota's state bird. My son Tony has his sons in tow. "Arms out and shut your eyes!" he orders, dousing them with mosquito spray from head to toe.

The Deep Woods OFF! is handed from one family member to another like a baton at a relay race. We stand armed for battle against the blood-thirsty mosquitoes as we grab our blankets for added protection. With anticipation, we settle in our lawn chairs for the grand finale. My husband Jim and brother John are setting up the homemade cannon shooter.

Jim, a mechanical wizard, built the cannon by using a four-foot steel tube robbed from an idle farm implement, sealing one end and mounting the contraption on an above ground support with legs spread-eagled. John fills a shot glass with gun powder, emptying it into the cannon's barrel. He stuffs scrunched up newspapers inside it, using a short pole to tightly pack the "charge."

"John, don't aim that cannon near those electrical lines," I warn him.

"Don't worry, I won't. You always worry so much."

As John lights up a match, kids and adults alike cover their ears for what is to come . . . the loudest of any fireworks in the area. KABOOOOM! The deafening blast bounces off the river and adjoining lake and echoes over and over and over again. Oh, yes, that was a good one. All the dogs have left for the next county—a sign that the sound decibels exceeded those that any animal can endure. As one cannon display will never do, John continues to shoot the cannon again and again to celebrate yet another Fourth of July.

I retreat to the cabin where the women have congregated, having given up their battle with the mosquitoes that joined forces with coveys of gnats.

"Girls, I expect a squadron of firetrucks to arrive any time. I'm sure some neighbor has heard these sonic booms, and thinks my cabin has exploded."

I rattle on, "Is that the sound of sirens I hear coming closer and closer? Maybe it's just the sound of my eardrums still ringing. John says I worry too much—but do I?"

Before anyone can answer, Matthew, my six-year-old grandson, runs frantically into the cabin, "Grandma, look over there by the river—more fireworks!"

I stand on the deck, and stare in disbelief. The severed electrical line crackles and pops as it dangles from the highland pole.

"John?" I ask into the darkness.

Nothing.

I don't ask again. My silence is ominous. I stand rigid, my fists clinched. I'm ready to explode.

Let the fireworks begin.

Poetry by Shirley Ensrud

Dress Rehearsal

There is a mess on the stage—
a bathtub, front steps askew,
trucks, wheelbarrows, backhoes,
piles of dirt and crushed rock.

I see the top of a head
and a hand as he slaps a trowel
full of cement onto blocks,
sets another onto them,
taps it with the trowel handle
to position it to his eyes' satisfaction,
then whips the trowel across
in almost ballet rhythm,
gathering cement squished out.

They raised the house,
gave the basement new walls
to enclose two bedrooms, a bath.

The drama is acted out daily—
different characters dig, wire, plumb;
actors make plans and do manual labor.
Intermission is nighttime—sometimes late—
and next day back on stage.

Our front-row seats are next door, soft;
view across our garden and manicured lawn.
We welcome the integrity of their performance,
look forward to the premier—
hope we are invited inside.

Poetry by Marlene Mattila Stoehr

Fall's Fleeting Splendor

Tallest of all, the pious spruce
remain aloof, unchanging, oblivious
to the firestorm of color below.
Feathery, yet green, tamarack
and stair-stepped pyramids of pine
provide a sedate October backdrop
to masses of maple and oak,
their leaves afire with an internal blaze,
their crimson hues crackling,
their branches intertwining
with yellow leaves of birch.
The landscape mimics
an array of luxuriant carpets.

And Nature, having created
this annual show, will, so soon,
lay these patterns on the forest floor.

Poetry by Don Haugen

faceless pleasures

funny thing

i tried to think of you today,
    i couldn't see your face.

my mind caught you for a moment,
    but it wouldn't hold and you were gone,
        i couldn't get you back.

i don't believe i can bear to think of you,
    it hurts too much,
        i have buried you deep
            so you can't escape.

brief startling iridescent images
    flash through my mind,
        betraying my conscious efforts to forget.

the fleeting images of your face
    are a torture to my soul.

        i have lost you,

            you are gone forever,

i love you so.

mercifully,
    your face is irretrievable
        to my mind;
            i remember only
                the faceless pleasures
                    of your soul.

Poetry by John Thornberg

Dangedling Modifier

Hanging there in midair
beneath a bridge to nowhere,
I wonder whatever became
of the dangling modifier.
Always on the hunt for a hook
from which to hang himself,
this suicidal maniac is as lost
as the proverbial fountain pen,
by a man, full of purple ink.
Where to look for a homeless
misfit in search of meaning,
who starts a sentence and fate
twists his words against him?
An island to himself, no man is
willing to brave the riptide
of academic scorn heaped on
him and those who attempt
to harbor such a castaway.
But who is at fault after all;
is not the sentence to blame
for not following the lead
of a well-meant phrase?

Poetry by Kathleen J. Pettit

At Twilight

Let's talk, then, just you and I.

Tea or coffee, perhaps a glass of wine,
and a fire flickering in its place
will set the scene.
You lightly brush my spine with tentative fingers
then slowly open my cover with a lover's
savoring anticipation.

I will talk of loves lost and loves dreamed,
of words never spoken,
silence between spaces,
commas between words, quiet nights,
bird songs and ordered words,
as if words could order our lives.

I will tell you of sorrow and pain,
    of laughter and joy, and

You will say, "Yes, I recognize that,
I have felt that, I know that,"

Or you will say, "I don't understand,
what nonsense, get over it."

And at the end
when you close my cover,
will you throw me aside as if I were an
old dream, no longer of any use?
Or, will I become a treasure,
something to come back to
at twilight when you feel most alone?

Poetry by LuAnne White

Baby Girl Gone

Quiet now—boxes waiting.
Yellow dog, Fluffy, her fur curling new,
keeps her eyes shut.
Baby doll faces the wall
so she won't see.
Rattles and nuk-nuks under the fleece,
orange and blue fish in the mobile
see the crib
Empty.
Left behind
no longer eyed or grabbed
each alone—desolate.
Baby's toys wait for a new home.

Editor's Choice Poetry by Marsha C. Porter

Levee

She wondered
  when her children had simply
gotten used to it—
  grief, *breaking*,
all through the house, soaking
  the sun-faded cushions
of the couch on the upstairs porch, running rivulets
  down the sheer red curtains lofting in breezes
through opened French windows.

Grief watermarked
  the dining room table, stained
the oil paintings, splattered
  the computer keyboard, dripped like ink
from a fountain pen, leaked
  as she tried reading the *Times*.
Grief slipped down her cheeks
  while she struggled to help her daughter with math
   homework.
Her daughter didn't say a word.

Grief slid secrets over the edges of the bed,
  onto the hardwood floor, slithered
down steep spiraled steps, and underneath
  the front door, into the moonlight's sonata, wanton,
as blues.

She pressed the tears to her skin
      with the palm of her hand and just—kept—going,
the way of those the world over who lack grief's luxury—
      place.

She remembers sitting
      at night
in the porch's slinky dark,
      late,
wondering why night
      was the only place she felt grief calm.
Dark, that
      held her,
 close as rain.

Fiction by Donna Trump

The Bridge

Joe Glover saw the ad in the morning paper. "Bridge for sale," it read. "Assembled steel bridge with wood deck; 4' wide by 50' long or other configurations. Best offer." He'd found what he'd been looking for.

On the youthful seller's ten-acre plot, the steel-framed bridge arched low from one wide bank of a silty Mississippi tributary to well past the second shallow bank. The southern Louisiana landscape was flat and green as a fairway.

"River's just not what she used to be, or so they tell me," the kid said, with a spit of tobacco juice. "Why have a bridge when you can step right over the darn thing?"

"Couldn't agree more," said Joe. "And here's my offer: I'll build it any way you like when I return it."

"Now, that doesn't sound like much of a deal to me, Pops. Can't you see I got no call for it any more?"

"Think you'll never need getting over something, young man?"

The seller tipped his hat back on his head, taut cheeks filling as he chewed. "Fair enough," he said.

In the morning, Joe called the garage and told them he wanted some time off. They'd known about his son and Jean for months and cut him a little slack. Joe filled the lock box of his truck with his best tools: full sets of ratchet and Allen wrenches, a few hammers, several pliers, a sturdy pry bar, his faithful power drill. Then he drove back out to the bridge. He loosened each bolt, took apart each cross strut and labeled every steel beam in waterproof black marker. He logged them all on green graph paper and in a 1:10 scale drawing measured carefully with a folding rule.

After a week of long summer days, Joe Glover had the bridge disassembled. The old pick-up sang at seventy-five miles per hour across Texas. Joe drove straight through, returning the salute of Saguaro cacti and spilling down the Arizona plateau into still-desert eastern California.

He found the place without much trouble, GPS-located months before by his son's last cell phone call. Jean had memorialized it with a cross and some fake flowers in high, matted brush a few yards off the freeway, but it hadn't been enough. So Joe borrowed the bridge, hauled it 1800 miles, parked the truck off the shoulder of I-10, and set to putting the pieces back together.

At dusk of the last day, the single-file passage rose and fell in shadow on a brief path parallel to the interstate. And even though the sun was setting neon pink over unfamiliar mountains and his every bone and joint ached from the labor of the last several weeks, Joe Glover stepped up onto the slatted wooden walkway of the bridge, one hand on each warm steel handrail. All that work and it only carried one person at a time: well, he would get Jean out here next. Joe measured a few more paces, bounced a little on worn-out legs and knew the bridge was sturdy enough. Then he strode up its gentle ascent, over the cross and flowers and it was as if he could see it, the future his boy saw that final night: the living, speeding, streaming red tails of the cars ahead, lighting his way down into the dark green valley.

Poetry by Joni L. Danzl

Hearts

Blood-red sumac pods tremble,
dangle from branches,
their velvet coats threadbare.

Crows' wings slice the sky.
Ice shadows,
gale winds gather,
up under the clouds somewhere.

The storm rattles
  the cores,
  the wings,
  the delicate husks of things.

Bloody anger!
Swollen bells and bitter seeds
throb as the wind rises.

Wings plummet.
Fibers fly.

Bloody pods spin
from branches,
detach and die —
their riddled hearts
spread finally
on the ground.

Poetry by Neil Dyer

It seems ill-timed to pose the question

now as the second glass of Pinot opens
up our veins. One never knows if an
afternoon like this may come again; the heat
painting us with a mortal calm, bees mustering
inebriate on the phlox beside the bay. The
answer you crave is achingly intuitive. We
have come far, you and I, far enough
to know that what has gone before is
incorporeal, a scarf of wreckage draped
behind us like a long forgotten tail. How
many seashores have I sown with salt?
Would it startle you to know that one
day I simply woke up and withdrew? It
was a greener time and I was as fuddled
as the bees. *So much bruised.*
Now the breeze lifts a shine of
perspiration from your perfect upper lip.
Your beauty is destroying me. Now you
know. But you must realize it was never
meant; it was done without intent.

Fiction by Jennifer Eudocia Sue Messenger

Ice

Snow so white it was almost blue rested on the branches above him. The water in between the small, snowy islands, the snow itself; everything glowed but the dark trees standing so tall he had to squint to see the top of their canopy. He did not glow either; his head hung as heavy as the wet snow he feared might fall on him. Rocking softly in the small boat, he put his head down and closed his eyes. There was almost a moment, then, when the bliss of dreamless sleep almost seemed possible, but as his muscles sank into the weight of his body, and his eyes stopped fluttering, the slow moan of dark beasts resonated gruffly into his ear.

The oppressive whoosh of owl wings beat steadily in the air just above his head, while the roar of a thousand tiny squeaks approached his sleep on the wings of bats. The man did not dare to look up or even open his eyes; he simply held his head tighter and once again replayed the scene in his mind, the night these monsters began to chase him so far from his home.

The weather had just been beginning to warm after a torturously long and bitter winter. During the day, melting snow had created massive puddles, while at night those puddles turned into glistening pools of ice. His body remembered so clearly how smooth it had been, how his car slipped out of control and seemed purposely to slide into the blinking light of a bicycle. There were moments of clarity and confusion after that, but it was the thunk of contact that caused this rift between two worlds and let out the monsters that followed him wherever he tried to escape.

Poetry by Marilyn Wolff

Gloom

On gloomy sunless
mornings such as this,
I crawl, slug-like,
from my bed
to puddle around the house
doing chores
that form the least resistance.

Shuffling through the day,
I slouch on the couch,
clutching the remote,
my thumb
the only sign of life.

Honorable Mention Fiction by Bonnie West

One Side of the Vase

He tells her a mistake has been made. But before he can explain, she turns to a woman, a sister or a friend, standing a little behind the hospital bed unwrapping yellow tulips, and says she knew there was no cancer.

The irony isn't lost on him and with the thought, his mind drifts, as it sometimes does, to his blunder on the SATs years earlier, when he incorrectly defined irony. Had he drifted off when he copied the notes from her chart? Reviewing it this morning, he saw the original information written in clear, perfect script.

Her friend smiles and looks at him for confirmation while holding the tulips sideways over the sink.

His patient turns back, laughs, begins clapping. Surprised, he reaches over quickly to press her hands together, to stop her delight.

Claire. He remembers her name as he releases her hands. He stands straighter. She is wrong. The cancer is still there. And, he says, there is something else.

Driving back to the hospital alone, he explained it over and over, so clearly. He rehearsed it riding up to her floor in the elevator. He'd been sure he'd act professionally, but instead he finds himself awkward in front of this high-spirited patient.

He never noticed anything, in particular, about her in the brief consultation the week earlier, but he sees now she has light brown eyes and a child's line of freckles across her nose although she is in her forties.

He sees her confusion at what he is saying. He thinks the friend must understand though, since she stops what she is doing and drops the flowers in the green glass vase leaving the red rubber band still wrapped around the stems.

He never wanted to be one of those doctors who saw the same

patients time and time again, learned all kinds of unnecessary and sometimes unsavory bits of their lives, and then one day had to tell them bad news while they stared, not understanding, frightened, hopeful. He'd become a surgeon so he'd rarely have to deal with that and here he was, where he never wanted to be.

He knows he has no bedside manner. He knew it before his wife left him, telling him he had no bedside manner, no in-bed manner either. That he was inattentive to her; he was always inattentive. And then all her things were gone, her navy coat from the front hall, yellow sweater from the closet, piles of dog-eared books from the bedside table.

He wonders, as he looks at the pale, confused face of Claire Williams, if the day he made the mistake, had he been thinking about his wife, about her saying he was inattentive?

Her friend moves, he thinks at first towards him, but then he realizes she is moving closer to Claire, as if to shield her from him.

Then he says it. "We removed the wrong kidney."

Sometimes you can see a person thinking, realizing, panicking like a child surprised by anger when praise is expected.

When he was four, he pulled a chair across the room and climbed up to the mantle to get the smooth round jar. He'd taken it outside, opened it, and dumped it in a puddle by the stoop. He was making mud pies and looked up, laughing, offering one, but his mother was slamming through the door, screaming about his dead father, grabbing up the jar and slapping his face.

Claire's face mirrors both his shock at the slap and his mother's horror.

How do you tell someone you've removed the good kidney and left the cancerous one inside?

She closes her eyes.

Her friend takes her hand, but she pulls it away.

He waits.

She doesn't open her eyes when she asks, "Can you put it back?"

He tells her the kidney cannot be replanted. He begins to explain about sterilizing agents and pathology but she is looking at him now, and he realizes he's saying it all wrong. He knows his wife could have said it better. She was so kind in the early days, protective of his inarticulateness, his preoccupied nature.

Claire doesn't take her eyes off him, but he glances away, around the room, to the friend who has moved to sit on the side of the bed, to the sink, a thin stream of water still coming from the faucet, to the flowers bunched and leaning to one side of the vase.

The look on Claire's face makes him offer an alternative, a transplant, he tells her. He does not say, although he knows, it is unlikely with cancer patients. He cannot help himself.

He leaves the room knowing he will come back later in the night, while she sleeps, to take the tulips and snip each stem, to make them last.

Poetry by Peggy Trojan

Inheritance

Two photos. One, Maria standing.
Her hat, large, beribboned,
black like her dress. One hand
on her sitting husband's shoulder.
Looking past the camera lens to end of ribboned hats,
beginning of childbirths, long homestead days.

The second, with three children, five more coming.
Husband seated, holding the newest baby.
No hat, hair pulled tight. Not smiling.
Wearing black, buttoned to the neck.

Her little domed trunk
lined in pale flowers with removable tray,
with the round bar of French soap kept in the dark.
In the wrapper these hundred years,
still smelling like lavender.

A short piece of crochet,
dark wine, made from leftover wool
used to knit mittens or scarf.
A note, "From Mother's petticoat."

Sixteen assorted buttons in a tiny glass jar.
Another note. "From Mother's dresses."

A small remnant of pine,
Nov. 5, 1915, written in ink.
Salvage rescued by my mother, nine,
as she watched Mr. Bottila and Father make the coffin.

These few, and Finnish grit in my blood.

Poetry by Dawn Loeffler

Instinctive Vision

I have seen you before
That crooked smile
That sly little smirk
Those slightly slanted eyes
Sparkling, foggy, mischievous
I know that swagger
That dip of the hip
Those shoulders squared with
Confidence, determination.
Wait, "What did you say?"
Oh, yes, I know that too.
How is it possible
Since this isn't you?
I have seen you before
On a shore of chocolate-covered sand,
In a mall up east
Where the rain slides forever in the streets,
On a plane you sat, heavily absorbed,
In a book, with a spine!
I was on the way to you again
At a pier watching surfers
In the mist of the sunrise
Pink above the eternal waves of the west.
You were in a grade school
Full of miniatures waiting to be you

At the grocery store in an aisle of cereal
Looking for coffee
With rich fragrance and bold flavors
At a stoplight in an economy sub compact
And again through that intersection
Riding a souped-up, huge-tired, flashy Dodge pickup.
As different as sprinkles or candles
On my birthday cakes
Not related yet the same
Similar yet not singular
As obscure as the years
That pass with difficulty
As regular as the days
That play the usual.
I have seen you before, and will again.

Poetry by Moose Malmquist

The Bewitching Hour

There is a fleeting time
at the very close of day
just as the sun begins to slip
into the purple valley of night
when for a few brief moments
a sense of quiet reverence creeps
across the woods and waters
as the sound of our loud voices
the collective rumble of our footsteps
and the growl of our machines
begin to fade and die
I then may hear
if I am very still
the gentle whisper of small wings
and the birds' muted evening songs
holding my breath I listen
for these voices
and for the footfall
of God's other creatures
whose hidden lives surround our own
who may now appear in all their grace and beauty
for just a fleeting moment
At the close of each day
to reaffirm their existence
thankfully sharing with us
a deepening sense of the wonder
and mystery of this earth
we sometimes think we understand

Poetry by Audrae M. Gruber

Brief Encounter

Shades of red, yellow, orange,
Sun-lowering twilight,
Tall shadowy evergreens,
End of a warm autumn day.

Through my window,
I saw you motionless.
Your confused and questioning eyes
Soon narrowed into fear.

I gloried in the temporal ridges of your perfect face,
Ears tipped high on alert,
Your Olympian strong neck and hard, slim body . . .
The recognition of "human," "run," and off you went,
Your shaggy, white-tipped tail bouncing in retreat.
Little did you know what joy it was to see you.

I am the intruder, not you, gray fox,
On this piece of land where you once roamed and mated,
Chased cottontails,
Gave birth and nurtured your young,
Townhouses now stand.
Paved paths in place of favored animal trails.
The wind whispers stories
Through the planfully planted pines and briar.

This manicured, park-like place where I live,
Lush, green, chemically-treated grass is mowed every Tuesday,
Watered every morning.
"Humans" walk only on black-topped paths and paved streets.
Bewildered deer, fox, and rabbits wander aimlessly at night,
Refugees from nearby woodlands.
They are a connection with a world now gone but never forgotten.

Poetry by Larry Schug

Great Gray Owl

The footprints I've left behind me
in twilight-blue snow
have followed me down deer trails
criss-crossing in this silent bog
where I chance upon a dead owl,
a great grey owl, its feathery cowl
frozen solid in ice at the base
of a naked tamarack tree,
its bones gnawed by mice it once hunted,
its flesh reincarnated;
its owly call now a coyote's howl
or a crow's raucous yell
singing a song of death become life
that wakes someone up
like a poem crying to be written.

Honorable Mention Poetry by John Thornberg

North Face

Lying here beside you
after a long day's climb
on the sheer north face
of a misty cold shoulder,
I am crafting a love note;
not in the ink of despair,
but bearing on its lines
whole worlds of longing.
We share one mountain,
negotiating its hard sides
of assent, inching down
the steep chasms where
agreement cannot go.
This terrain of marriage,
the topography of which
both mystifies and thrills,
has left me stranded again
on the heights of hope
searching for the pathway
back to my valley of dreams.
Lost in your clouds of sleep
you do not know how deep
my need for your touch.

Fiction by Kathleen Lindstrom

Inside and Outside

He's sitting next to me, but he's not really here; he's lost in his head somewhere, wondering how to tell them, what words to use. I know that's what he's thinking.

I turn to look at him, but he doesn't notice. His right arm is braced against the steering wheel, his eyes focused on the road. So I watch the land go by instead. It's bleak this time of year, all beiges and browns, blacks, patches of snow here and there, trees in the distance, their bare branches lying like lace against a white sky, fields falling off the edge of the earth. How lonely it is. So endless. How can people stand it out here?

I smell his cologne—Old Spice, something he's used since we met. He's a creature of habit, after all. There's something safe about that.

He's wearing the sweater his mother brought back from her trip to Ireland, which itches and makes him sweat. So he only wears it when he visits her. I can smell the wool, or maybe it's the dust from our back-hall closet. Or maybe the dreariness of our everyday life.

The car is stuffy. It's been a long ride. We're almost there.

She greets us at the door, looking older than her sixty-one years, shorter and paler. She's wearing an apron, with BIRD IS THE WORD embroidered on the bib. The smell of turkey wafts over me like an ocean breeze. I realize how hungry I am and, all of a sudden, how glad I am to be here. She falls into his arms, whimpering with joy. She hugs me. She urges us into the living room, then heads for the kitchen to bring us coffee.

Walter ambles into the room, shakes our hands, asks us how the drive was, turns on TV. They forget I'm here and quickly focus on a fat man who is yelling out football statistics into the camera.

I sit in a soft, high-backed chair starting to feel uncomfortable about my jeans, having chosen them to make a statement—to let them *know*. But let them know what? What was I thinking? They have holes in the knees and rips up and down the leg. My sweater is stained and shapeless and I've tied my hair into a ponytail. It's limp and needs washing.

But she doesn't notice and is kind to me, inviting me into the kitchen where it's warm and we can do some serious *woman talk*, she says—let the men watch their old football game.

She does all the talking, and it's about some new pie recipes she's trying out for the county fair, hoping to win her sixth ribbon in a row; hoping the price of eggs will increase so she'll make a profit this year; hoping the drought has finally ended and they'll get a decent crop for a change; hoping Walter's arthritis won't force them into a retirement they can't afford; hoping the worst is over and God will send down the grace I need to . . . .

She has that look in her eye, ready to say more, but I tell her I need to pee, then stay in the bathroom for as long as I can, studying her fish motif on the walls and towels and shower curtains until my husband knocks on the door and tells me it's time to eat.

I sit across from him at the table, grateful for the large turkey centerpiece she made, which has huge feathers and blocks him from my view. I wonder if she planned it this way. But he sits up higher, trying to find my eyes, looking for signs in my face.

He asks about their health and their neighbors and their little trials and tribulations and how they're coping with the weather and the economy and the wars and the rest of the world. He listens to them and shows concern. He gets them talking about their aches and pains and their dos and don'ts and the daily nuisances that can drive you nuts. He is their only child, after all.

He's getting them ready for our news, I can tell.

Still, the memory of our little girl surrounds him like a fog, filling the room with clouds and rain, making it hard to breathe, making it hard to find any words.

I remember when we met—him asking me to dance, bending at the waist, extending his hand, kindness in his eyes. My friends laughed at him, a farm boy in a white shirt with a string tie, bowing and being so polite. We were celebrating someone's twenty-first birthday, I think, and chose this small town dance hall as a lark.

I stumbled in his arms, couldn't figure out the polka step-hop-slide, and stomped on his feet a few times. But his eyes just crinkled up and he chuckled — a low murmur in the back of his throat that got my attention and made me study him more closely. Actually, he was a good looking guy. Tall and thin, sandy hair, shirt sleeves rolled up, showing off some muscle.

And . . .

Our little girl cried constantly and we couldn't figure out why. The pediatrician attributed it to ear infections, common at that age. But when the fevers wouldn't go down and she wouldn't eat, he ordered tests, then referred us to a specialist. She has lymphoblastic leukemia, that cold woman told us; you have a tough road ahead.

Then . . .

I always wonder why she works so hard on these get-togethers. It must have taken her hours, maybe days, to get ready, to cook all these dishes from scratch, then to see them devoured in twenty quick minutes. Now our men are rising from the table, scraping their chairs, patting their bellies, burping their appreciation — surrendering to the lure of that new big-screen TV in the other room.

He didn't tell them. Maybe he lost his nerve. Maybe he's waiting for his apple pie.

Toward the end, she'd lost half her weight, her hair, her smile, her will to live. I wouldn't leave the hospital (couldn't), thinking my presence would make her better, make her want to live, take away her pain.

He would come after work, white as a sheet, searching for something hopeful in my eyes, disappointed when he couldn't find it, getting angry sometimes. She left us for good on a Tuesday night — her body sinking into death with a long, rattling sigh. I watched the pain lose its grip on her face, her eyes opening up half way, her mouth forming a little smile (I'm sure of it). Then I saw a drop of water fall on her cheek and looked up to see where it came from. It was my husband, who was leaning over her and crying.

I knew then I couldn't live with this man any longer.

Don't . . .

She's made three kinds of pies—pumpkin, apple and pecan— knowing which one each of us prefers. I'm not hungry, but feel compelled to eat anyway. The light in the sky is fading to gray and I know we have to hurry this up. He doesn't like driving country roads in the dark.

But he's playing with his whipped cream, lost in thought, worlds away on the other side of the table. They seem to be waiting, knowing something big is about to happen here.

So he lays down his fork, stares at the linen tablecloth, clears his throat, and begins to break the news. "Carrie and I . . . well, it's been an awful year, as you know; and, well, it's been hard on both of us, on our marriage. So we've decided . . . "

"No!"

My outburst startles everyone, including myself. They turn to stare at me, their eyes dark and round, like wells.

"Don't!"

But then I have nothing else to say. What should I say? So, I get up and head for the bathroom again, locking myself in. I sit on the toilet seat, rocking back and forth, trying to get my bearings, trying to figure this out. I study the rainbow-colored fish on the shower curtain, looking whimsical and stupid at the same time.

I remember reading something about fish. It was a symbol for the early Christians, I think. Something like that—that fish were filled with water on the outside and the inside. Was that it? That love is everywhere—inside and outside—all at the same time. Even in death. Even when we're drowning.

Especially then.

Is that really possible? To be lifted up and loved at our worst? I'll have to find that book.

I hear him approaching the bathroom, his footsteps tentative and soft, letting me know he's coming. He's good about that, alert to what I need and how I respond to things.

He stands outside the door and listens for a while, figuring out the best way to do this. Then he knocks. And then I let him in.

Poetry by Elizabeth Eva Lampman

This season

i always slip
on the icy vestige of you.
panic and clamor
my arms reach
for invisible support.
when i exhale

i am still standing,
planted yet attentive,
and step forward cautiously.
by the end of the winter
i'll have learned how to tread on memories
without losing my balance.

Poetry by Kathryn Kirmis Medellin

A Walk with My Father

Weeds and grass
covered the plot
of land that once had
been his garden
cosmos, lilies and daisies
had grown there.
His walk was not that of
yesteryear
straight and tall
walking with
purposeful stride
through his garden
stooping to
pull a weed
pick a flower.

What thoughts were his as he
struggled to make his legs
carry him past the
weeds and grass—
his labor that brought
exclamations of delight
admiring glances
from those who passed by?
Thoughts about
working the soil
planting seeds
signs of growth
pushing through the ground?

Tending his garden
through the summer
first frost of fall
winter months
searching catalogs
planning for spring?

I walked with him
that day
a silent walk.

Fiction by Catherine Ritchie

The Garden

"Mr. Martin?"

It had only been a week since my father's funeral, but I was startled to hear his name.

"Who's calling, please?" I asked.

"Grayson's Landscaping. We have the tree that he ordered, and our crew could plant it tomorrow, if that would work for you."

"I, um, Mr. Martin died recently. This is his daughter, Meg. I don't know anything about a tree being ordered."

"Oh, I'm sorry! I didn't know." There was a pause. "He paid in full for the tree. What would you like us to do?"

I was curious. "What kind of tree did he order?"

"Ginkgo Biloba—this one is a beautiful tree."

I thought of my father in the final weeks of life: silent, withdrawn, restless. Wandering the neighborhood, spending hours in the backyard.

The salesman respectfully waited out my silence. Then he added, "Mr. Martin said he wanted it for Emily's garden."

I nearly dropped the phone in shock. Emily, my mother, had died six months prior. Feeling unexpected tears, I sought to end the conversation. I wrote down his phone number and told him I would call him back.

Emily's garden? Dad had said nothing about this to me. Hanging up the phone, I went out into the backyard. There was no garden, per se, only clumps of weeds and wildflowers around the edges. But over toward one side, I noticed something new—a pile of rocks and small boulders had been pushed into a rough circle. The ground had been cleared there, enough, I supposed, for a tree to be planted.

A strident meow around my ankles announced the presence of the gray tabby cat known as Tabbit, so named due to a grandchild's inability to pronounce "Tabitha." She had been my mother's cat, and as my father's love-hate relationship had developed with the animal, he was often prone to grumbling, "Dagnabbit, that Tabbit!" But when he thought no one was looking, he would reach out his gnarled, rough hands and gently scratch between the gray ears.

Such was my father—gruff, angry exterior; quiet, private interior. And there lay the dilemma—which side was present on any given day? I had learned at a young age to always approach with caution.

Looking farther in the yard, I saw that more rocks had been laboriously pushed into a rough circle around the old rose bush. Some of the weeds had been hacked out, but far more remained. Like so much in my father's life, he had simply run out of time. So many regrets, so much left undone, unsaid.

I'm sure he had loved my mother. He just couldn't say it. Maybe it had been different when they were younger; I'm told he even took her dancing a few times. The later years had been more strained, more harsh between them. When Mother finally died, it seemed to me as though, emotionally, she had left long before. It was only a matter of time before her body joined her spirit.

I looked around at "Emily's Garden." It wasn't much to look at, but I could see the beginnings, the rough edges my father had shaped. Was this to be a tribute to her? Or an apology?

Tabbit shot off after something hidden in the brush. I watched her go and remembered the odd little dance she would often do around my father's feet. Tail twitching, eyes flashing, she would try to tackle his shoes—the fierce predator attacking her prey. Dad would usually just ignore her.

"What you looking at?"

I was so deep in thought, staring at the backyard, that I hadn't heard my brother Mike arrive. We were beginning the process of clearing through the inevitable "stuff" left behind when someone dies.

"Dad ordered a tree for the yard," I explained. "I think he wanted it to go there." I indicated the rock-ringed area.

Mike's face turned ugly. "A tree? What the hell did he do that for?" Mike and my father had barely spoken to each other over the last few years.

"Something about a garden for Emily."

Mike spat. "Yeah, well, it's a little late for that, isn't it?" He turned around and headed into the house. "Like everything he ever did—too little, too late." The door slammed behind him.

I winced, more at the words than the noise of the door. I could certainly understand why my brother felt the way he did. Dad was simply not a nice guy at times. Growing up, Dad had treated his son exactly the way his father had raised him—harsh discipline, no coddling. I had been spared some of that, simply because of my gender. I suspect that Dad, never having had sisters, had no reference guide for how to raise a daughter. He had left me alone, mostly, referring me to Mother whenever I had questions.

But I was tired of the anger. Perhaps Dad was too, at the end. The tree, the garden may have been just a gesture, a last-minute attempt to mend old wounds. Dad wasn't here to say. But I was.

Entering the kitchen, I watched my brother stormily toss things into boxes, or into the growing "junk" pile. Anger is a poor family legacy, I decided. Picking up the phone, I dialed quickly. "Mr. Grayson?" I said. "Plant the tree."

Weeks later, I stood once more in the backyard. The house was in the process of being sold, the "stuff" had been cleared out, and Tabbit and I had come back for a last visit. "Emily's garden," or "Sister's lunacy" as my brother referred to it, was much more visible. The newly planted Ginkgo tree was clearly the crowning glory, holding stately court over the rejuvenated rose bush, with peonies and lilacs encircling the yard. I had added a few touches of my own—a crimson barberry hedge that represented my father —functional, but sharp-edged. And for Emily, my mother, mounds of geraniums, her favorite plant, filling in the spaces around the tree and the back stoop. It felt good, standing there, seeing the promise of the garden in full bloom. It felt right, inside, with no words to explain it.

Out of the corner of my eye, I saw something shimmer. When I turned to look at it directly though, all I could see was the Ginkgo tree. As I was puzzling over what I had seen, Tabbit shot past me into the garden. Meowing loudly, she raced toward the tree, straight toward the place where I thought I had seen the shimmer. Tail straight up, twitching madly, she began to pounce and twirl around in a circle, as though trying to catch something.

Tabbit dashed back toward me, rubbing against me, still meowing. As I bent to touch her, I sensed again the shimmering near the tree. Though I could see nothing there, Tabbit immediately ran back to the spot, and again danced around in circles, as I had seen her do so often with Dad's shoes.

I stared at the tree, my heart pounding suddenly. Tabbit stopped her wild pouncing and sat still, as though invisible hands were stroking her. I imagined old, rough hands gently scratching her ears.

"Dad?" The word came out hushed, almost choked. I blinked back tears. Though I could see nothing there, there was a sense of someone, of something, in that garden. Was I just imagining it?

A gentle breeze wafted through the backyard, stirring leaves and aromatic blossoms. The cat stared up at the tree, as though listening to the wind. Then she turned and walked back to me. She purred loudly as I bent to pick her up, and she continued to purr in my arms, rubbing her chin against the side of my face. I stood there for a few minutes, stroking the cat, staring into the garden. Waiting for . . . something, I suppose, a sign?

Tabbit struggled to get down. When I obligingly placed her back on the ground, she licked her fur off briefly and walked off around the house without a backward glance.

I found myself smiling. "You're welcome, Dad."

Poetry by Frances Ann Crowley

Thinking of You

As I flip through a seed catalog on this cold February day,
I'm attracted to the loud-pink face and easygoing charm
of a Bourbon rose. He hangs out all over the place
shooting the breeze with his sprawling, boisterous buddies.
The propaganda says he is intense and dense,
highly ornamental, and armed with prickly thorns.
My olfactory memory translates "sweet fragrance" into "smells
    like trouble."
My inner custodian screams "high maintenance."
But he is so lush and happy. I know he will light up the
    darkness.
He is definitely my type. I must have him.
I will bring him home and coddle him and care for him,
even when he loses his petals and makes a big mess
he doesn't even notice.

Poetry by Patricia Conner

The Way Light Falls

For Mimi

The way light falls aslant in early morning,
exaggerating sheen and shade,
sharpens the agony of yearning.

Out in the day's routine, our senses churning,
we can attend to duties, even evade
the way light falls aslant in early morning,

painting her pillow, gilding her cup, and turning
sofa and soft quilt folded into knife blade
that sharpens the agony of yearning.

Always we seek the answer, but this learning
provides a truth we do not want replayed.
The way light falls aslant in early morning

recalls the way her song and laughter, burning,
lit up every room and every crowd.
This, too, sharpens the agony of yearning.

Yet, though we never want this scene remade,
we sing to her glowing, that will never fade
in the way light falls aslant in early morning,
a light that sharpens agonies of yearning.

Poetry by Marion C. Holtey

Rainbow Footprints

She sits on the rug with her doll
choosing pieces for a picture puzzle.

As the sun shines through prisms of a tall
cut glass window, she points to tiny
rainbows on the rug. *I wonder who left
the rainbow footprints* she says and looks
at the soles of her small white sandals.

They aren't mine she says, examines
my feet, the dog's and every corner of
the room. *It was an elf* she decides and
sits down again as the rainbow footprints
walk across the puzzle and her tiny legs
while she giggles with three-year-old delight.

Poetry by Cheryl Weibye Wilke

Keeping Time

The bubblegum-pink alarm clock sits
on a night table marking time
for an eight-year-old.

The bells on top squat frozen.
Its old-telephone ring silent.
Two glow-in-the-dark hands move

at will around the wheel. Rarely,
if ever, on time. And she's okay
with that. After all, what is time

to a child? A brush of blankets. Touch
of snow. Stroke of midnight, only to be
rushed with a wish for tomorrow.

On the other hand,

I'll keep time however I can. Frozen.
Silent. Whimsically moving in the dark
to mark her every breath.

She *is* time.

Poetry by Sharon Harris

Mother to Child

I feel like
you are my heart
now outside
of my body

somehow when
you were born
my heart
became you

I will never
feel whole again
unless
I am
holding you

*Note: This is an editorial board member as well as a member of the board of directors of the Jackpine Writers' Bloc. This work, and all work in the book by the editorial board members or board of directors of the JWB, is not eligible to go to the celebrity judges or receive prizes.

Poetry by Jane Levin

Squash

I walk between rows of threshed corn stalks,
stubble on morning's sleepy face.
There is no give beneath my frosty boots.
This parched Minnesota land
 has given all she could.
At row's end,
the land yawns open
to fields of withering umbilical cords,
once lifelines that nourished a field of multi-hued squash.
Which seeds were hastily sewn
into seams of threadbare coats,
traveling steerage across the Atlantic?
Which were stowed
in tiny earthenware jars,
buried in Arizona internment camps?
How many perished on the journey?
I squat to caress
forest green globes,
plump tans, streaked with teal,
orange and yellow turbans,
blood-red tear-drops,
promise to raise the next generation.

Fiction by Harrison Hicks

Seeds

John dreamed, but it was not quite what he had hoped for. People lingered at the edge of his unconsciousness, bending over the borders at odd intervals to whisper an imperative, "Find your silence . . . . " Restlessness stole the sleep from his eyes . . . and they blinked open to sunlight staring patiently, certainly down at him.

He sat up, and the blankets tumbled off his torso. Bugs clawed at his eyelids, hanging onto his face for dear life, and red spiders spun their red webs around his blue irises. Inertia fell with a thud and the clinking of chains, dragging at his ankles as his legs meandered their weary way to the floor. It was a day just like they all were in Leominster, Massachusetts. He trudged barefoot across his room, across his house, across his town, to the general store and leaned like a sack of potatoes against the apple barrel. He pulled one out, tossed two pennies to the clerk, and walked back to his house, waking as he walked, as he munched.

It was all he knew, this place. This town was his world, his paradigm, and he did love it. But his dreams no longer let his existence remain as it was. He looked at the floured faces that poked out of kitchen doors with a cheery "Beautiful day, Praise God, Johnny!"; the faces on porches that held pipes limply in their lips and nodded a greeting; the buildings that leaned against each other like families; the dust that held it all together like the ties that bind. It was beautiful, and it was no longer enough.

That night, he dreamed of apples but he didn't know why.

He woke up again. Funny, it seemed more like a bad habit than a natural cycle now.

Signs went up that day, all over town. "Land Out West!" they cried, pleading behind a bravado that spoke in fonts a bit too large to be credited. Manifest Destiny might not be enough on its own . . . .

The clerk was muttering to the Reverend in the store that morning. "T'aint Godly. I've seen the folk that's headin' out there. They're sending all the convicts out there's what they're doing . . . and the heathen Injuns . . . just ain't Godly, Rev'rend . . . Mornin', Johnny . . . . " The Reverend nodded sagely in agreement, and offered a quiet greeting to God through John. When their eyes met, he felt his mind's eye twitch. Why was he so dry, so hungry, while the Reverend satisfied his soul on the words of God that came out of his mouth? Was it a sin of pride that he couldn't be lulled to sleep by tales of searching people more sinful than he? He didn't know.

And the townspeople smiled at him, greeted him, loved him. And John loved them. But . . . ? And but why?

That night he dreamed of black, glossy seeds in a bag, and a man walking across America. Each step brought him closer to himself. He woke with a start, and the whispers of his dreams lingered and echoed for a minute more . . . it was close now.

While walking on his bare feet to the store, Johnny saw the Jensen boys tumble out into the street, laughing. He smiled to see them, so unconcerned, so fulfilled. Was the secret to be found by wrestling in the dust of a simple street with the ones you love? Almost, but he hadn't any brothers.

In the store, he bought three apples with six pennies. Looking down at them, he smiled. If there was one thing that he knew was good, that he loved without question, it was a juicy, red apple. Who could question it, needed any more of a why? It's an apple. You eat them; they taste good. He walked out of the store, up to the Jensen boys. "Hey guys," he said. Joe let his brother out of a headlock and they stood up in front of him, grinning. "Have an apple," John said, and tossed them each one. Not because it was a beautiful day, not to praise God, but because he loved the boys.

John walked the long way home, past the Butler's farm. There was Mr. Butler in his field, throwing corn into the sky, into the sun to bake and pop and grow and be. Was it a destructive joy, to discard and discard until there was nothing left? John watched, leaning on the fence, almost until the flightless tumbling seeds germinated and extended their leafy green fingers to the blue heavens and yellow star. No. It was a sacrifice, made for someone else.

That night, he didn't sleep. He stared out his window and let his dreams whisper through the starlight, a silver murmur that called and caressed. A few minutes later, the stars turned their faces eastward and hushed.

Shrouded in scarlet secrecy, the Sun began to rise from the East. It whispered to John.

"Follow me."

He followed it into town as the people began to wake. He followed it past Butler's farm, where the seeds still slept. He followed it past the store, and bought an apple, some apple seeds, and a pot. He followed it past the Jensen's house and peeked in the boys' window. They were just waking and laughed in their beds when John made a face and put the pot on his head. He walked on, and kept it there because he didn't need a reason to.

The Sun rolled on, stretched itself in the growing morning light, and yawned. It turned to look behind at John, who dropped his apple core on the side of the road. The Sun smiled, and John smiled back. The Sun crested and headed West.

"Follow me."

Somehow, that was all it took.

Published by the Jackpine Writers' Bloc

Poetry by Marianne McNamara

A Midsummer's Night

He brings a sack filled with good things:
a jar of pickled okra, vintage Irish cheddar,
Lavash flat-bread crispy with sesame seeds,
tomatoes still sun-warm from his garden.
Armed with plate, knife and basket
he mounds crackers, slices tomatoes,
lays out gherkins and cheese.
I contribute sepia bottles of icy cold beer.
The breeze picks up but it's still too hot.
I hold the chilled glass against my forehead,
lift my hair, let the air cool my damp neck.
Easy together, we laze in the backyard beneath ancient oaks;
eat, drink, laugh and tell stories until the slow arrival
of darkness is complete and the fireflies click on.

Poetry by Alberta Lee Orcutt

At the Birdfeeder

The Red-Bellied Woodpecker
doesn't have a red belly

Finches, chickadees, grosbeaks—
even the haughty blue jay—
all give way to him, all
intimidated by this painfully shy,
smartly handsome
Red-Bellied Woodpecker

        dapper stripes with orange vest
        brilliantine red head

I know a woman whose flaming red hair
enters the room before she does:
Her blue serge suit and silk cream blouse
are so classy
women in silver lamé twinge with regret
—even as they are drawn to her

        her lilting voice
        her fresh soap scent

Poetry by Andy Johnson

winter fruit

my window disobeys
the rule-of-thirds
taking focus
off the woman's eyes
allowing her
maybe walking to the dry cleaners
to slip into the background
before she disappears entirely
leaving me with the stagnant
layer of snow that
encrusts the sleeping ground
like an orange peel
waiting to be pulled away
so she can take a bite
its juice will stain her
clean white blouse
she'll take it to
the cleaners tomorrow

Honorable Mention Fiction by Vern Thompson

The Organist

Alma Nordquist walked up the steps of a small white church beside a poplar grove off the gravel road. It had been her church for fifty-six years, and for fifty-five years she had been its organist. Alma usually came on Wednesdays, but this week she had decided to practice on Tuesday. She unlocked the front door and made her way through the entry to the small organ in the back of the sanctuary. A dozen pews on each side of the wide aisle led to the simple altar; and above it, between two small stained-glass windows, hung a large rough-hewn cross—a sacred relic saved from the frontier log church of the 1870s.

On this cloudy afternoon, the church was nearly dark. Only faint light came through the stained-glass windows, and the shades of the side windows were drawn. She was reaching to turn on the reading light when she heard muffled sounds coming from the front pew—low rustling, heavy breathing, and then deep groans. Who could possibly be in a locked church? Only three people had keys: Einar Peterson, who did some janitorial work, Pastor Bob, and Alma. Pastor Bob came out from town only on Wednesdays for confirmation class, never on Tuesdays. It had to be poor Einar, perhaps having a heart attack.

She started to rush forward but stopped stock still. Amid the heavy breathing came, unmistakably, the garbled, higher tones of a woman's voice. Alma felt her knees begin to buckle, and she struggled to catch her breath in little gasps. She crept out through the entry and silently locked the door. She sat for several moments in her car, staring at the church. Sex! In her church! Fornication in the house of God! She leaned her head on the steering wheel to keep from fainting.

Finally, she was able to back slowly out of the parking lot. She drove aimlessly down back roads, trying to control her thoughts. Who could it be? Not poor Einar. She almost laughed at the thought. Pastor Bob? Who was the woman? She drove past the church again, knowing what she had to look for. Down a grassy lane into the grove, almost hidden from the church and the road, sat two cars. She immediately recognized Pastor Bob's black Buick. The other was a red SUV with an American flag on its antennae, and then she knew.

"Marge Anderson," Alma said aloud. "Our Marge Anderson! Having an affair with Pastor Bob! In our church!" Sweet Marge with flaming red hair and two girls in elementary school and a handsome husband who rented part of their farm and worked at the Eagle Ridge lumberyard. And now an illicit affair with a preacher. It was just too much for a seventy-five-year-old woman. It was as if all the old values were slipping away. All of the settled things that should be in place were changing.

And the church itself was changing. Hers was one of the last struggling country churches, a dozen or so families spread among empty pews for worship, now relegated to Sunday afternoons to fit the schedule of Pastor Bob's larger congregation in Eagle Ridge. Worship itself—the hymns, the quiet ritual, the old verities of The King James Bible—all seemed under attack. And she knew her position as the only organist was in danger too.

It had all started innocently enough with a wandering group of earnest, fresh-faced young people, carrying, they said, "the gospel of Christ in song." Well, that, Alma knew, was highly questionable. The atonal music, filled with wild riffs and flourishes, blasted through electric guitars, drums and huge amplifiers. Two young women in short skirts and shockingly low-cut blouses gyrated and twanged through breathy lyrics, incomprehensible except for an occasional "Jesus" and "heart" and what sounded like "graaaace." Alma was appalled to see many in the congregation, even her husband Ed, nodding in time to the roaring, pulsing beat.

After that, the church council decided that one service a month would be what they called "contemporary." More drums and guitars came from their own young people. Even elderly neighbors brought out banjos and fiddles. Even, for the love of God, an accordion. So once a month, Alma was forced from her organ bench to join Ed in a back pew. The old blue hymnals stayed in their racks. Songs were handed out on mimeographed sheets or, worse yet, projected on a screen at the front of the church. It reminded Alma of the old movie shorts when audiences sang popular lyrics projected on the screen—following the bouncing ball like a bunch of slow-witted, tone-deaf rubes. Alma's rich, confident alto was reduced to a low murmur as she stood while her back ached and the congregation galloped through simplistic stanzas and endlessly repeated choruses and shouted requests for just one more. She fumed at Ed, "We might just as well close up and go over to the Pentecostals." Ed was non-committal.

And the preaching, if one could call it that, had become spiritless and insipid. Instead of lessons from the Biblical text, it all hinged on "warmth" and "sharing" and "saving the environment." She couldn't recall the last time she had heard even a mention of original sin. She knew of several members who needed a good "straightening up" and no one in the pulpit to do it. Did seminaries nowadays turn out nothing but ninnies? The last three had been spineless ninnies; and now there was Pastor Bob—a spineless, adulterous ninny.

Tension between Alma and Pastor Bob had been building ever since he had shown up for his first women's Bible study in Bermuda shorts and sandals. The crisis had come on a spring Wednesday as she finished practice. He bounded toward her, spilling over with good will and bumptious enthusiasm. "Dear Alma," he boomed, "practicing after all of these years." Alma looked steadily at him over her reading glasses as his confidence drained away. "I really think—I mean we think—you deserve to retire—after all these years." His upper lip began to quiver. "God is saying, 'Rest now, Alma, thou good and faithful servant.'"

Alma still locked him in her gaze. "I don't think we can presume to know precisely what God is saying about anyone—least of all me. I choose not to retire."

Pastor Bob gave it one more try, standing beside her and gently stroking her shoulder as he bowed his head. "Lord," he prayed, "help dear Alma to accept changes in her life."

"Lord," Alma prayed silently, "take his hand off me, or I will stand up and slap him." He retreated, but Alma knew he was already pushing the church council to ease her into retirement.

And now this had to be dealt with. She pulled into the farmyard and sat for a long time in her car. She would do her duty. She would reveal all to the church council. She would demand action from the Bishop. The whole community would be in an uproar. And then? And then. The chain stretched on inexorably. Marge disgraced. Possibly a divorce. The little girls shuttled back and forth. Pastor Bob's career destroyed. For the first time in years Alma wept, her slim body racked with deep, shuddering sobs.

Finally, the sobs quieted, and she looked resolutely out past the barn and the fields of ripening corn. She knew what she had to do. And she would do it.

For several Tuesdays, she drove past the church and saw nothing. Finally, she spotted the cars and let herself silently into the church. As she sat down at the organ, she again heard rustling and heavy breathing. She drew a deep breath and slammed her hands down on the keyboard.

The old organ roared into the opening chords of "Great is Thy Faithfulness." Above the music, she heard a woman's piercing scream and caught a glimpse of two figures silhouetted against the stained glass windows as they flung themselves wildly toward the side door.

Alma played on through the lengthening afternoon, the grand old hymns rolling out the open door and across the pastures and the shadowed fields.

On Wednesday, Pastor Bob submitted a vague resignation. The next Sunday, he preached a rambling farewell sermon. As he finished the benediction and started down the aisle; he glanced at Alma, seated straight-backed at the organ. She held him in a steady gaze over her reading glasses. Before he managed to look away, she offered him a thin smile.

When she was sure the congregation had reluctantly joined hands, she swung into "God be with You 'Til We Meet Again." Marge would salvage her marriage. The seminary would, no doubt, send out some other ninny; but Alma could handle him. Three Sundays a month were enough. Alma Nordquist was at peace.

Poetry by Jean Childers

Break-in

The winter has slithered into the house.
Behind the door molding, water has
gathered, and drips in onto the wood floor.
I hear this unfamiliar sound—a soft *plop*,
and think, what else could happen? What more

can I give I haven't already given?

Still, the intruder creeps in, tries to break me.
I will keep the invader at bay the best I can,
with towels and my heart laid at the doorstep.

Poetry by Renee Loehr

Alzheimer's

Which side of the bed do I sleep on?
she questioned as she entered her bedroom of forty years.
As she crawled into bed fully dressed,
I reminded her she didn't have her nightgown on.
That's okay — these clothes are fine, she replied.

Wandering back and forth between the couch and the bedroom
Not sure where she belongs.
Coming and going with no purpose.
Making another trip to the bathroom,
forgetting she had been there only minutes before.

Picking up an empty glass,
refolding a blanket,
trying to remain useful,
to feel some sense of normalcy.
Knowing, yet not knowing what's happening.

Not able to follow a conversation,
responding inappropriately,
fabricating her answers so quickly I'm amazed.
Insistent on getting her questions answered
with answers that make sense to her.

Sweet and gentle one moment,
angry and aggressive the next.
Not remembering what she ate for breakfast
but recalling vividly nurses' training sixty years ago.
A lifetime of memories locked in a mind with room for
        no more.

Creative Nonfiction by Louise Bottrell

Shopping in JCPenney's with Grandmother Maude, Circa 1945

"Yeeees, this is my little granddaughter, Louise. *Say 'hello' to the nice lady, Louise.* What did you say your name is, dear? Hmmmmmmmmm. I knew some Augusteins over near Pana. Would you be related to the *George* Augusteins? They're upright, hard-working folks, and it was a shame the way they lost all their land in the depression, but I've heard they are doing very well nowadays in the flower business. Pana is the rose capital of the world, you know. No relation, you say. I'll tell you, Mrs. Augustein . . . oh, well, *Bertha* then, if you insist, and call me Maude, please. I'll tell you, Bertha, my Luther and I almost lost our farm, too, so I can sympathize with those who did. If I hadn't written to FDR—President Roosevelt—we never would have saved the farm. He intervened *personally*, you see. Well, it wasn't as if I hadn't corresponded with Franklin Roosevelt before. Our birthdays were on the same day. I sent him a birthday greeting every year on January 30 and *always* received a response. Luther says the letters are typewritten by FDR's secretary, and I suppose he's correct, but *signed* by President Franklin Delano Roosevelt, mind you. *Let go of my sleeve, Louise, we'll be leaving in a minute.* I was heartbroken when he passed on, that dear man. I called my daughter Helen—that's Louise's mother—the minute I heard the announcement on the radio. We cried as though a member of our own family had expired. Oh gracious, Louise is getting restless. Well, my dear, it was so nice meeting you and having this little chat. *Louise, we're almost ready to go. As soon as I get Bertha's phone number, we'll go over to Kresge's and buy you a Nancy Drew book.* I really suspect Louise has sinus trouble, Bertha, and it makes her nervous sometimes. I'll just jot down your name and phone number. I'm a Perfection Wax representative, and I believe you'd be interested in our wax. I coat every door and every piece of woodwork in my house spring and fall. It just sparkles! I'll be calling you, Bertha."

Poetry by Sharon Harris

Morning Glory

my mom and I
plant
one packet
of morning glory seeds
every spring

it is our unfailing
ritual
something we do together
every year

she is ninety-three
I worry and wonder
how many more springs
we will get to do this

in the store today
I spotted a display
of flower seeds

in sudden desperation
I plucked ten or twelve packets
of morning glories
from the shelf
and hurried to buy them

Poetry by Debbie Pea

Grandma's Diamond Ring

She often told me it would be mine someday
and I always changed the subject.
I couldn't imagine her ever leaving me.

I told her I was glad
she was not a rocking chair grandma.
She told me there's too much to do.

She divorced two husbands and
outlived three. And she still managed to find
some years in between to live contentedly alone.

She lost two sons but never lost hope.
I marveled when she described the mysterious peace
that settled on her shoulders at their funerals.

She traveled around the country
until she was in her early nineties.
She wrote me letters and told me secrets.

She played piano and cards and games.
She baked and sewed and studied and read
and told jokes and prayed and went to church.

She taught me lessons (or tried).
Once she told me that people are stupid enough as it is
without drinking alcohol and making themselves stupider.

(I always think of that
when I am in the middle of
making myself stupider.)

One day at work I listened to the voice mail message:
"Grandma died today."
My tears were mixed with a mysterious peace.

I wrote a poem for her memorial service.
Later, when I slipped her ring on my finger,
it fit me perfectly.

Creative Nonfiction by Deb Nelson

Closet Memoir

I held the first of the moving boxes closely, standing in my new apartment and gazing at the hallway closet. The small space was empty for now, but it would soon be filled with the spoils of shopping wars, the shadows of childhood monsters, and shoeboxes full of memories bound onto glossy pieces of paper.

The move back to Minnesota had gone as smoothly as could be expected—my entire life fit into my little car—and the hunt for a place to live had been quick and painless. The second I'd seen the familiar-looking closet, I'd known that it needed to be mine. Lions, witches, ghosts, and magic lurked inside.

After setting the box on the floor, I wrapped a hand around the cold doorknob and pushed the door open, half-convinced I would see the crowded space of my parents' hallway closet rather than the vacant shelves I knew were really there. I could almost see it: unused rain coats on one end, canned vegetables piled in the corner, and the window air conditioner left on the floor until it was needed in the summer.

A young girl perched on the air conditioner, snuggly wrapped in a decades-scuffed quilt, a flashlight and a book in her hands and the real world pushed firmly from her mind. "What are you reading?" I asked softly.

I imagined her looking up at me, blue eyes nearly black in the darkness, and I watched her silently smile and hold up the book's cover. "That was one of my favorites," I whispered before I had to blink and the closet stood empty again, my past flitting back into memory.

How many times had I read the same books growing up, flipping through the pages again and again, creating and destroying worlds within my mind until I no longer needed the books to tell the stories? How many times had the flashlight failed, leaving me to read words I couldn't see, the story continuing to play out in my head to the beat of an unseen melody?

Stepping into the closet unleashed memories I had long since thought forgotten. I pushed the door closed with my foot and gazed into the calm darkness, dusting my hands over the shelves and feeling a smile creep onto my face. Here there was no one to bang on the door and demand to know what I was doing and why. Here there was nobody but me.

It was perfect.

"Do you remember?" I asked the shadows trapped in the corners, wondering how many spiders were sharing my recollections, "the first time I put down my books and picked up a pen?"

As I spoke, I could almost hear the distant chatter of the television and the sounds of my family, could practically feel the frantic way my fingers had gripped the pen as I scribbled out barely legible words. Characters had danced for me, universes had flowered in my mind, and epic adventures had unfolded exactly the way I wanted. So full of smudged ink and hopes and dreams, that first notebook had filled too quickly—followed by a second, a third, and a fourth.

"I wonder where those notebooks ended up," I murmured, old memories brushing against my mind like spider webs. A deep breath slipped out of my lungs to chase them away as I felt for the handle, letting the coolness of the metal seep into my fingertips.

Lingering a moment more, I slipped out and picked up the box of kitchen supplies. There were more containers to cart in, wrinkled clothes to put away, an air mattress to locate, and my computer to set up. If I didn't want to sleep on the floor and wear these clothes again tomorrow, I didn't have time to stand in the warm gloom of a closet and daydream.

One of the boxes from my car opened to display an old, tattered quilt, lovingly folded and placed on top for the move. I pulled it out, wrapped the patchwork throw around me, and glanced towards the closet. "Perhaps I could buy a chair," I mumbled, thinking about all the time I had spent sitting on that old air conditioner.

I smiled as shadowed memories peeked their heads out from the closet and beckoned me forwards. Flowing stories begged to be written, scheming characters darted from the darkest places in my mind, and pen and paper clamored for attention on the kitchen counter.

I shook my head and carefully set the quilt aside for later, digging deeper for my air mattress. I could write later; for now, I had to move into my apartment.

"If I do get a chair," I muttered as I finally yanked my air mattress from its confines, "it's going to be a lot more comfortable than that old air conditioner ever was."

Poetry by Suzanne Cecere

Sunday Afternoon Bouquet

One sleeping cat, curled in corner of couch

One person, preferably self, lying on couch,
bare feet resting on compliant sleeping cat

Sprigs of open windows, light breeze, flapping shades
The steady hum of a distant lawn mower

Fill with assorted bird song and dappled sunlight

Dreams, not quite ready to open

Honorable Mention Poetry
by Audrey Kletscher Helbling

Hit-and-Run

In that moment, I know,
as the rivulets of water course down my body,
as I step from the tub
dripping puddles onto the linoleum,
that the sirens wail
for you,
my boy, my only son.

You, who tossed your backpack
over your bony shoulders,
then hurried
toward the street,
toward the bus stop.

While I showered,
you crossed carelessly,
your fragile body bouncing
off the car
you had not seen,
flailing in a somersault,
landing hard on the pavement.
Sirens scream, and I know.

Panic grips,
holds tight my heart,
my very soul,
as I race from the bathroom,
wrapped in a bath towel,
stand immobile,
watching the pulsating red lights
of the police car
angled on the street,
blocking the path to you.

Poetry by Andrew Scott Browers

All the Way to Earth

I went back in time, just a bit
And I plucked from a night sky,
—we stood together beneath it, marveling—
a star. It fell to earth that night,
and left a trail of breadcrumbs
or starcrumbs
or whatever sort of crumbs a star leaves for its friends,
to follow it wherever it goes
Even to the earth

It was falling then,
but I went back there and I caught it,
held it in my hands

"This," I said, "is a lucky star."
And I divided it in half,
and put each smaller star in your eyes—just a fleck, really—
Where they could burn like sapphires
forever and ever

And they would always bring you luck
And they would always leave a trail of stardust
So you would never get lost

Not ever again.
Even if you fall
all the way
to earth.

Poetry by Dennis Herschbach

Youth

The pendulum moon swings
between full and empty,
golden disc to inky nothing
crossing off month after month
with the stroke of an eternal pattern
that was, that is, that is to come.

I don't count seconds or minutes
or even hours. Days blur,
the decades heap up
memorials of memories
that accumulate with each tick
of the grandfather clock
standing forty-some years
in my dining room corner,
its pendulum journeying
from one side and back again
in a relentless rhythm
marking one theft after another.

Time, a silent burglar,
sneaked in unnoticed,
and one night I looked out my window
across a snowy landscape
broken by twisted shadows
of tree limbs reaching up,
praying arms entreating the moon
to give back what was taken.

Creative Nonfiction by Kristin Laurel

Easter

It was an expensive ham, apple-smoked, slow cooked. Yet, it left us all sitting in the living room with indigestion. I see the worry in my oldest son's eyes. My daughter is offering to wash the dishes. Only my youngest son and nephew seem unaffected as I watch them across the street throwing freshly dyed Easter eggs at each other.

We talk of the weather. The sky is stuck in gray in Iowa today, like it's undecided.

Outside on the dirty grass, a half dozen robins chirp. Mom asks, "Where do robins go in the winter to get so fat?" She talks about the old basswood tree that shades the deck. "It's dying on the inside, but looks so healthy on the outside." I think of Easters past, how the passage of time ebbs and weaves away at our years. I recall a time when my kids were younger, when they were excited to find a plastic egg full of candy and didn't steal the change out of my purse. I remind them all of the year my youngest was crawling around the yard, and I saved him from putting a frozen piece of dog poop in his mouth.

I look at my step-dad. He's all spiffed up today, standing there steady and strong leaning against the wall. He has pain in his back, but he's too proud to take up room and spread out on the couch.

Every thirty minutes or so, he pulls a dropper of liquid morphine out of his front pocket and dabs it into his mouth. He talks of chemo, radiation, how the cancer has spread to his bone. He's pretty relaxed and looks content; maybe it's just the morphine. My mom looks old and worried. I rub her shoulders, tell her I can make her knots go away. Ken says, "Hey, can you rub my cancer away?"

My sister is talking about buying a fiddle. She's been listening to her "favorite" song by The Charlie Daniels Band — "The Devil went down to Georgia." There's no talking her out of it. We all agree to help her buy a fiddle, even though last year she was fixated on fish. She bought all of my kids a Tetra for Christmas; one of them spilled out in the car when we tried to take it home. I remember I had to grab it while my son screamed, "Save it. Mom, save it—give it CPR." I ran upstairs, threw it in a glass of water, and it lived until the cat ate it.

My littlest sister wants another baby. She's been on fertility drugs —and every time she starts her period, she brings home another horse, or goat, chicken, dog, cat, or rabbit.

This is my family.

I go for a walk. I see an eagle nesting in an old oak at an abandoned farm. Everything's symbolic. I go back to the house and find a dead black bird in the front yard. What does this mean?

I look for a shovel, but not very hard.

I take the gutter off the house and dig a muddy hole, tell my mother I clogged the rain gutter, can't get it back on the house and to beware of the shallow grave that is now in her perennial garden.

We say our *see ya laters*; we don't say goodbye. I drive off with a piece of pie on the hood of my car, watch it fly to the road in my rearview mirror. My kids start to argue whether one of them was really sick last week. My son says, "You can't fake the stomach flu."

It's strange, this slow way of dying. Everyone I've known that's died has gone quickly, like blowing out the candles on their own birthday cake. I don't know which is better, but I hope I go quickly or I'll think too much. I have myself a good cry, feel a little better . . . like maybe I'm going to get through this stomach flu.

I call Ken up. It's so like him to make me feel better, when he's the one dying. He tells me he loves me, that he will always be with me. We talk about Mom, how she's been through hell, how her first husband tried to kill her, second one killed himself, and now he's dying.

Then he says, "She's a strong woman, but you better watch out for her when I'm gone."

I ask, "Where is she now?"

"She's out in the backyard cussing out God, demanding another Resurrection!"

Poetry by James Bettendorf

North Shore Drive

There are places
you must stop
Gooseberry Falls
different every time
a trickle   then a rage
feeding the lake
near the shore basalt
rises out of the waves
ready to tear at hulls

on calm days you can lie
in yellow light
on the flat black face
imagine voyageurs
gliding by in canoes
paddles dip and swish
the sleek prows split
the surface

the long climb
up Eagle Mountain
through mosquito-
insinuated swamps
tripping and sliding
on the rock-covered path
you see deer on the trail
white gulls above black crows
the occasional red-headed
turkey vulture soars and hunts

if you're lucky an eagle
fox or even a wolf

and Split Rock Lighthouse
just like on the postcards
if you stand on the beach
look at it against the blue
     sky

it is in these icy waters
I can tolerate only
for a few seconds today
I tell my children
to spill my ashes

Poetry by Richard Fenton Sederstrom

Aspen

Here's how well we work together, not always,
Understand, but most of the time, especially
When we're not paying attention.
When we came across the aspen
That the morning's unweatherly
Tornado had spread broken and naked
Across the drive, I didn't have to say a thing.
"We'll get the chainsaw," she said.

I limbed out the broken trunk while Carol
Dragged the gangly pieces into the woods.
Then I cut up the body of the tree, and we
Both finished the job. And it is only now,
When she and I are—well, only a couple
Of towns apart, and only for the rest
Of this week—it is only now that I have used
Words like *body* and *limbs* and *naked*
And maybe especially *gangly*, when—

I have all but given the downed aspen
A name, that I know that I am somehow
Being trained for grief. I read yesterday,
Was reminded, that Elinor Frost died
When Robert was just my age. Elinor
And Robert had been married just as long
As Carol and I have. His lunatic grief
Left him as helpless as the aspen spread
Out in the woods at the side of the road.

We work together in such company as that,
Carol, I, the aspen and our histories, the constant
Work to revive the fallen in ourselves.

Honorable Mention Creative Nonfiction
by Lyla E. Owens

Mandatory Fun

Rest, to cease from action or motion; relaxation, the act of relaxing or state of being relaxed: a lessening of tension. Rest and Relaxation (also known as R&R), a military program that provides a three day break in a noncombat zone for all deployed service members. The modern version of R&R is a cruel practice. Three days are only long enough to relax just enough to remind you that there is another world beyond the bubble that you now live in and until someone gives you permission, that world is off limits. You are in the suspended state of limbo, between two worlds, between two selves. You have three days to try and forget that you are not in charge.

When on R&R everyone wants to forget where they just were, to ignore what they will have to go back to when their three days are over. In Qatar, over 300 complete strangers try to act "normal" and fail miserably. We, all the service members sent there, tried to pretend that we were on vacation, everyone avoiding the reality of the situation. Our world was a false world, like carnival season, when everyone masquerades as what they secretly want to be. We just wanted to be civilians and, for three days, we all were.

There were still rules in place to remind us all that we were still in the military and to keep us safe from ourselves. This was not the wild, unsupervised R&R of my grandfather's and my father's time. Though we tried to pretend otherwise, our time there was very controlled and regulated. There are public images and diplomatic ties to maintain. If we were going to cause an incident, those who were in charge ensured that it would not be easy for us to do so.

Every individual was allowed to have only three alcoholic drinks a night. After nearly a year of sobriety, we were all lightweights and for many of us one and half beers was enough. Our base was in a conservative Arab country, so our attire had to conform to their standards. That didn't matter because the only time we wore our civilian clothes was to and from the pool, and at the bar. When the sun went down, the rules were let up a little and the females were able to show a little more skin. Above all else there was to be no fraternization between males and females, unless your spouse happened to accompany you on R&R. Everyone there was confident that that rule was meant to be broken. During the daytime, we all behaved respectfully towards each other; we acted oblivious to the sexual undertones that were present in everything we did. It was only after the sun went down that we became men and women instead of males and females.

Night time was our time, but Big Brother still had to remind us that in the end he manipulated and controlled us. Though it was dark, the base was lit up everywhere, so that privacy and anonymity were next to impossible. They were trying to force us to remain in the light, thinking that that would stop us or anyone from acting like normal men and women. Every light post was like the giant eye from The Great Gatsby; nowhere was safe from his all-seeing gaze that could penetrate the shadows. In our search for privacy, we became slithering nocturnal creatures, moving quickly, skirting the light, seeking the safety of the dark. When we found it for a few brief moments, we were safe from the light and the prying eyes; we were only men and women, and we were only a man and a woman.

We could not hide from reality forever. On the third night, we all numbly stood before each other, unsexed in our uniforms, identified by only a last name and our rank. Everyone made feeble attempts at joking and trying to seem as if they didn't care, but we were all just going through the motions. Our minds were already gone from R&R as we were thinking about our units and what awaited us when we returned. When the flight manifests were posted, we could no longer prolong the inevitable. There were rounds of handshakes, hugs, as we all said our goodbyes. Here and there, couples claimed the corners for their own goodbyes. Those who could not find a corner stood in the open, no longer caring who saw. No one would have done anything about it anyway. With heavy feet, we all shuffled to our planes. It was only a formality; we were already gone.

Poetry by Tara Troge

The Return

Where have I been?
Away for so long,
back from the depths
of the unimagined.

Tears of new life
fall down an old face;
I've missed you my friend,
what did you sacrifice?

My voice, my peace,
my soul, my heart;
All of it for others,
carried away in parts.

Poetry by Doris Bergstrom

On the Dark of the River

Three clumps of light flutter
on black waves,
weaving their reflections
earlier and earlier as
winter pulls evening into night.

One bright candle flame
flickers passage to
underwater creatures,
scatters beams upward
alerting heavy-lidded owls

struggling to stay awake
for snow or no-snow report,
grumblings of the Congress,
status of our planet, and how
Earth Moon and Planet Mars
share space this night.

Those across the river might
gaze at our lights
(if they choose to look)
but for them evening ticks
early to bed long before
I close my day.

They may be six a.m. risers
rippling lighthouse beacons
on the black trail of the
river
calling dreamers to awaken
but I am not one to know.

I sleep into daylight
when the river yawns
reflects trees
shaking their branches
wide wide awake . . . .

Creative Nonfiction by Steve Linstrom

The North Shore

The waters of Lake Superior crashed against the dark rock shelf surrounding Isle Royale, jubilantly throwing streams of glittering white water diamonds into the air.

From our vantage point on top of the little rise across the bay, we watched our three boys cavorting across the hard crusty surface, dodging the splashes from the incoming surf and stomping in the sparkling little pockets of water. They looked like they were bounding across the face of the moon.

"Terribly brutal the way the Lake relentlessly pounds the Island," Sarah said, her rich dark brown eyes open impossibly wide. "Year after year it takes a little piece of it with each wave. It's terrible but beautiful."

She turned to look straight into my face. "And in the end—you know—Superior will win and the Island is changed forever."

"But the shore changes a little every day," I said, my fingers running up her spine. "Not all at once. And there is no winner or loser, only change. That's what makes it so beautiful."

She faced the bay again. "Not too close now!" she yelled, her loud mom-ish voice carrying across the water. "And keep your shoes on!"

I smiled. Our "boys" were 25, 23, and 13 and more than capable of watching out for themselves. A mother's instinct to protect is always there. As they have since adolescence, they pointedly ignored their mother's advice. Support her—yes. Listen to her—no.

"It's relentless and the end is inevitable," I said, as a large streamer crashed against the rocks and slowly faded back into the dark body of water. "In some ways it reminds me of . . . "

I could feel a small shudder from Sarah's back. Silence hung as I closed my eyes and lowered my chin to my chest. It was always there at the edge of our consciousness. "Christ," I thought as I shook my head. "Even here, I have managed to do it again."

I covered her hand in mine and she placed her other hand on top of it, squeezing tightly. I turned to look at her beautiful face and saw it was scrunched up into her famously ugly grimace. Sarah didn't cry very often, up until a year ago that is, but she cried the way she did everything else. All in, full out.

"I'm sorry," I said. "I didn't mean . . . "

"Just shut the hell up!" she said as a tear made its way down her cheek. "Don't you know we can't be afraid of the word?"

I put my hand behind her head and drew her to my shoulder, my fingers entwined in the thin wisps of hair the chemo had left us.

"Shhhh," I said as I stroked the back of her head. "It's okay. This Island has stood up to Superior for millions of years and we'll stand strongly too."

"I know we will," she said in a whisper. "It's just that I hate this freaking disease. It's just not fair and there just isn't enough time."

I wanted to tell her that everything would turn out okay.

I wanted to tell her that we had time.

I wanted to tell her that they might find a cure.

I wanted to tell her that it hit each person differently.

I wanted to tell her that some people lived with the Beast for years.

She knew. She knew it all. She had heard it all before.

I—can't—fix—anything.

I pulled her head to my shoulder and felt her teardrops wetting my neck.

"I know," I said. "And we love you."

Poetry by Linda Back McKay

Lake Effect

Now it is cold
by the lake,
colder at night
when a tree falls
dead, its birch
bark casket
flanked by
sheaves of reeds.
Here dandelions
flounder
in the yarrow.
Humming
birds will
not linger.
There, a moose,
his smoky
breath rising from
whatever burned
in him today.
It swirls
like secrets
the old ones
took with them.
Then the rocks,
the canted
black rocks
lure you
closer than
you'd ever
dare to go.

Poetry by Lindsy J. O'Brien

I bury my Self in January

Beneath a paper skin,
and frozen years looped, thin
my heart is still
green: Only the shrill
knock of the pileated might recall
me to my sap.

       A white shell
heaves the weight of the sky
over iced water but cuts away the shy
spider-shadows of sun:
Light, when do you come
again to set the backs of small
fish aglow in me?

       I almost recall
the dimpled purple of my
flowering. Now I lie,
brown and in darkness, stiff:
My someday curled, my what-if
what-may-be rooted firm
to black detritus.

       I learn
to forget my own
unfrosted breath: The lone
loon cry that recalls when
I know my Self again.
The Light loops and sings
and carries Me in its rings.

Honorable Mention Creative Nonfiction
by Dennis Herschbach

Tonight

According to my calendar, the moon will be at its fullest. The sky will be cloudless, or so the weatherman says. The snow will be illuminated even more brightly than it was last night, when through my rime-crusted window I saw sharp-edged shadows outlined on the frozen, white canvas of nature.

I will dress warmly: insulated boots, hooded jacket, wool-lined leather mitts and, sometime before midnight, I'll step outside. My breath will congeal in the air, forming micro-clouds of crystals that will sparkle in the moonglow. Then I'll lay my snowshoes on the corn snow, and it will crunch and squeak under my weight when I step onto their rawhide-webbed frames.

With unmittened hands, I'll fasten the leather bindings of the snowshoes behind my heels, over my boots' toes, and over my insteps. The brittle-cold metal buckles will burn my bare fingers, drain away heat, and make them stiff and unresponsive. But I'll tighten every strap before pulling on my mitts again.

The moon will reflect so completely I'll not need a headlamp or even a match to light the way, and I'll follow the trail that winds between balsam trees standing ice-coated, sentinels adding to the silence of my world. I'll touch the bark of a towering birch, its covering as white as the snow. In the moonlight, the bark's lined markings will be so black they will appear as if drawn by a pen held in the skilled hand of an ink artist.

There'll be no need to stop to cool down. I'll only stop to listen.

I know that somewhere in the distance a great horned owl will call his familiar question, "Who?" And I know that somewhere, possibly close by, a maple tree will split from the cold with a retort as loud as a high-powered rifle discharge. I know that I'll listen to silence so deep it will seem to swallow my world.

If I look for a moving shadow, I'll glimpse a snowshoe hare following its familiar path from den to who knows where, and I'll wonder why it risks the owl's talons by coming out on a night like this. I'll wonder if it must, as I must do.

And in the distance, if I am blessed to hear, a lone wolf will lift his muzzle to the nighttime sky. He will howl a lonely cry to the moon for no real reason other than he needs to hear himself lament to an unseen god. Last summer I saw his tracks in the red clay mud. Tonight, I'll ask him for a serenade.

But if I stand too long, my toes and finger tips will begin to ache, and I will have to move to cause my heart to pump faster, stronger, circulating warming blood from my body's core. My steps will be smooth and rhythmic across the crust of daytime melt turned solid by the arctic wave sliding down from the north.

The leather harnesses of my snowshoes will creak and groan as they rub on the varnish coating of their wooden anchors, and their cadence of complaint will be as mesmerizing as the swish of branches brushing my jacket sleeves. And then it will be time to make the turn at the end of the trail, to face the direction from where I have come, to reenter a world that continually draws me back to what is, I am told, reality.

I will slowly wend my way up the trail, and my house will come into view, first as points of light flickering through the tree branches and hazel brush, then as defined rectangles where windows act as beacons and, finally, as a hulking frame in the moonlight.

I'll look up at the dining room window, the one facing out back toward the woods, and I'll think I see her standing there, a cup of hot chocolate in her hands and a warm smile on her face.

I'll remove my mittens again, only now the temperature will be five degrees colder than it was when I left. In an instant, my fingers will stiffen and the metal buckles will sting more sharply than they did when I hooked them on. I'll step out of the harnesses and stand the snowshoes upright, tail end down, in a drift. I'll trudge up the stairs and welcome the warmth of air exhaled from the kitchen when its door swings open.

I'll put another log or two in the woodstove and watch through its glass doors as wisps of birch bark seem to spontaneously ignite. Then I'll pour myself a glass of wine, turn the lights down low, and look out the window at twisted tree limb shadows on the snow. And I'll remember.

Poetry by Christine Stark

Hope

She tore the second to last steri-
strip off the red stained, zig-zagged
doctor's cut from belly button to pubic
bone. She looked, for the first time, at
the cut that would be with her now for
the rest of her life and it stung and she thought
the doctor would have left a steadier
cut, not as uneven as a row of teeth
gnawing at her insides. She hoped,
as she has been doing for three weeks, that the
medical intervention would be the magic
she has searched for nearly forty years,
the magic of starting anew, of not repeating
the same mistakes over and over—a child at a
piano—*plink plink plank*. But her hope wavered, skin
stung, on the uneven, red-gullied marks of the doctor's hand.

Poetry by James Bettendorf

Clone

I carry an extra set of keys
in my pocket because I cannot
clone myself and stay in the car
when I leave for an errand and be there
to open the door in case I lock it
with the key inside and I would
be allowed to use the car pool lane
since there are two of me
or three in the car and it would count
as more than one person
if it were still only me
and I would not have to buy new
clothes because all my old stuff
would fit and I would never
have to be alone or would I just be
with myselves as I am now
my endless companion.

Creative Nonfiction by Jan Wolff

Recovery Room

Vicks VapoRub. Good for sneezes and sniffles, heavy chest colds and mothers' consciences. Also effective in transporting memory backward through time. I take one whiff and once again lie prostrated below the heavy iron headboard of a squeaky-springed double bed. It stands against the north wall of the overcrowded cubicle which, throughout my childhood, served double duty as my parents' bedroom and their children's infirmary. When illness struck, Mother tucked us into this first floor room, thus saving herself numerous trips up the steep flight of stairs to our bedrooms.

I feel again the totally occluded nasal passages and the dry discomfort of mouth breathing and I see the cracks across the fly-specked ceiling. Long ago white, its papered surface has dulled to murky beige and wears the streaks of numerous futile attempts at cleaning. At its center hangs a fluted glass light fixture, death trap of a dozen or so small insects which show through the milky translucence like random freckles, not to be erased until the light bulb has burned out.

On the walls pink roses perch, tethered by squares of intertwining blue ribbon, each square about six inches across. I have counted them all. Eighteen squares between north and south walls. Thirteen from floor to ceiling.

Beside the foot of the bed, and occupying the entire remainder of the east wall, stands a dark walnut armoire with a mirrored door on either side and six drawers down the middle. Above the drawers is a smaller, curved mirror which can wondrously transform the leanest of faces into a full moon. This piece of furniture serves as clothes closet, storage space, and catchall. Stacked across its top are bundles of old letters and business records, yellowing scrapbooks, photo albums, several hand-made Mother's Day greetings (crayoned or pasted onto bright construction paper), two men's felt hats, a can of buttons and pins, a kerosene lamp, an ancient and seldom-read Bible and a bottle of Sloan's Liniment which wafts its wintergreen aroma about the room, penetrating my swollen nostrils and reminding me, nostalgically, of Christmas candy.

Across the rug-strewn, wooden plank floor, and below the only window, stands an old-fashioned, treadle sewing machine. Its hinged cover is folded to one side and stacked high with ripped and torn clothing, mostly of blue denim.

On either side of the window hang what in 1945 were known as marquisette sheers, see-through curtains of a not-quite-tan hue, described by Sears catalog as ecru. Their uneven hems provide mute testimony to the inadvisability of home laundering. In deference to my illness, the dark green shade is partially drawn and pinpoints of sunlight shoot through otherwise undetectable openings, illuminating the dust motes that float through the air.

The sewing machine bench doubles as a night stand and brings within my reach the evocative Vicks as well as a black and white box of Smith Brother's cough drops, a tin container of menthol-scented salve with a colorful religious scene depicted on its cover, a bottle of aspirin, and a sodden handkerchief. A half-full glass of tepid water has made a white ring on the surface of the bench and is accumulating tiny bubbles along its inner sides. Except for the droning of a single fly, caught between window and shade, the room is completely quiet.

I turn restlessly onto my side, face to the wall. The sheet has pulled away from one corner of the mattress, exposing its blue and white ticking cover. I run my finger along one stripe. Up and down. Up and down.

The pillowcase feels cool against my cheek and gives off the intermingled scents of Dad's tobacco and Mother's hair. I am overtaken by a cozy sense of drowsiness and I close my aching eyes.

The fly drones on but I am soon asleep.

Poetry by Jane Levin

Wonder

Snowfall in Southern Minnesota
transforms every farm
into a cream-of-wheat field.
My '86 VW bus farts nonstop down Route 61
putt—putt—putt.
Drivers brake as they pass.
Blonde heads swivel,
hoping for a glimpse.
Who lives such memories?
I flash a smile like I'm totally stoned.
Eyes averted,
they scurry like roaches,
leave all the joy for me.

Published by the Jackpine Writers' Bloc

Poetry by Vincent D. O'Connor

Sonata

Sunset streams
in shafts of light
through cracks
in tattered window shades.

In a corner
palsied hands
make tender love
to polished spruce and ebony.

Quivering strings sow trills
that whirl and tumble gracefully
through the air
finally falling
to saturate wearied carpet.

For a moment
memories of concertos
echo
from empty walls.

Poetry by Laura L. Hansen

Confessions of an Emerald Ash Borer

Here in the dark, tucked
under the interlacing ridges
of bark, I can think of nothing more
than my need to eat, to feed, to be.

Here under the tree's stiff coat
I need nothing
of what the sun has to offer,
nothing, not yet.

Here in my pupae state, pale
and soft and free of any carapace
or shell, I feed, follow the runs
of sap as it climbs

the tree. My need is this,
this sap. I consume and move,
consume and move, leaving behind
long-looping scrolled & hidden notes.

So soft I move along the fibrous
wood, without color or spine, without
any god but this, this languid
cut and chomp, and these

paisley songs, my coming out.
I leave you now with nothing more
than my ashen signature
and doubt.

Poetry by Sharon Harris

Winter Cover-Up

snow melts.
the big banks shrink
in the ditches,
revealing
all kinds
of unsavory things
that winter had hidden.

a rib cage
of a deer
reaches up
like mute fingers
to an uncaring sky—
frozen delicacy
for neighborhood dogs.

Poetry by Viola LaBounty

Between the Doors

Today, unexpected breath of spring.
Warming temperatures
melting winter's ice and snow.
Afternoon sun basking on windows and doors.
I step out to check the mail.
Open door, scent of spring
captured between the doors.
Caused me to breathe in deeply.
No mistaking it,
Spring is on its way.

Poetry by Janice Kimes

Two Poems for Spring

1. The Robin

Tentatively you come
in this debris of light
to startle a faded silence
into song.

2. The Joke

Warm winds beguile us.
Each day becomes polyphony
of fair-weather friends.

The lace of budding life
adorns the trees, earth
molts brown, then doubtful,
then unquestionably green.
A unison tryst of promise.

Will trust endure the ridicule?
the day dawns white—
an April's fool.

Fiction by Sandra Edlund

Last Call

Neon lights flashed before her like a beacon, a lighthouse in the fog guiding a ship to safety.

"Come in. Come in," they seemed to say.

She knew if she went in, it would be warm and cozy, full of sustenance, eat and drink and that intangible other, companionship, warm bodies to hang with. A place where vagrants and vagabonds roost like homing pigeons resplendent in tatters and tales of humor and woe.

Ashes, flicked off her cigarette, dusted the sidewalk as she watched the patrons in the window, mouths opening and closing like buzzing insects, their faces glowing in wide smiles and laughter. Huddled together, they talked and drank and ate and she thought of herself as a kid sitting around a campfire pressing graham crackers around sticky marshmallow oozing sweet melted chocolate.

She closed her eyes and inhaled the smoke and it burned in her throat and she thought, *god I want a drink!*

No, you can't, she told herself. *You know what it will lead to. No job, no boyfriend, you'll lose it all. Don't go in!*

But the people in the window, they looked so happy and if she went in, she would not be alone.

She had tried AA but it was too much like church. You walk into a room with a circle of chairs and they hand you a book like a hymnal. You go to meetings where you read and pray and there are rules. Lots of rules. The people are nice and smiley and they hug you but only if you share and give away bits of yourself. And the people seem to want the dark stuff, the painful stuff, things that are buried deep inside. Things that you wouldn't tell your best friend. That's what these strangers wanted and she couldn't do it so when they all went out for pie and coffee after the meeting, she was left. Alone.

And when she tried to call someone from the phone list they gave her, the phone just rang and rang, so what good was it?

She wanted the noise, the music, the kaleidoscope carnival where she could lose herself and she wouldn't cry and she could be hap hap happy. And most important, she would not be alone.

The cigarette burned out and she crushed it with her heel. She started to shiver and closed the coat around her tight. She walked across the street, opened the bar room door, and she was gone.

Poetry by Scott Stewart

after hours

. . . the smothered cigarette's spirit
ascends
to a temporary heaven—
a dissipating charcoal haze
further dimming yellowed lights

. . . empty glasses conspire
in a darkened corner—
first chirping and chipping—
then singing—a chorus clanking
and clinking—serenading the
barkeep in a late night ritual
—yesterday's stale song—
—tomorrow's stained salute—

. . . sulking under the splashed dissonance
drifting across the bar's scarred mahogany
        the
last shot of rye
watches a hovering
 hand
    swoop
        in
            for the final
kill

on a gnarled battlefield of scratches, scrapes, and gutters;
a swamp of damaged straws, drowned napkins, deflected
        dreams;

                launched
                 from
            a tarnished stool
             squeaking in
              relief as its
                 rider
                 leans
                 into
               the trough

Poetry by Sheila Myers

Break Time

My dear friend, you have been missed these
past six months since you moved.

Remember how we used to watch the clock
waiting for break? Today, with the spring
sunshine blocked by the closed blinds, the
clock moved even slower. I went walking on
break today and imagined you with me.

We started the break by you telling me of an
annoying issue at work,
Then we swapped a couple humorous
stories of things our kids did lately,
We commented on how nice the sunshine
felt and were glad of the wind since it kept
the bugs away—though it could have been a
bit less,
We talked of how strange it was not to have
our other friend with us and then
speculated on how her trip was going,
I told a silly story of something my crazy
puppy did,
And you talked of your dancing students
and the next performance being planned.
Then as we neared the door, we dragged
our feet, since neither of us wanted to go
back in.

It was a good break; glad you could join me.

Poetry by Barbara Farland

Widows' Banquet

It's shortly before two on a Tuesday afternoon
When the gray-haired group toddles into the
    country-style diner
Known for its senior specials and pancakes.

The women, some stooped, one leaning on the
    arm of her fellow patron,
Claim a long rectangular eight-seater though
    they number only five
And hop their chairs up to the table.

Three appear primped for the occasion
With flowered tops, resin beads, heavily-scented
    dime-store talcum,
Hair coiffed tight in curls.

Two more scurry in looking disheveled and annoyed,
This gathering a seeming interruption to their
    afternoon in the garden,
Their twill pants bearing fresh grass stains.

A ceiling fan whirs overhead sending a chilly draft
    on the gaggle below
And persuades the one with a coat to lift it to
    and over her shoulders
As if caped queen of this widows' banquet.

Poetry by Harold Huber

Seventy-Fifth Birthday

Six a.m. Woke up old
Five and seventy years
Antiqued, dinosaurian
Fossilistic

Seven a.m. Not quite as old
Vertical balance regained
Hunger soothed, shaved, combed
Awaiting the postman

Eleven a.m. Mailbox stuffed
Limericks and love notes
Tongue-in-cheek jabs
Methuselah jokes galore

Two p.m. Hardly old at all
Brisk walk, juices flowing
Joints and muscles buzzing
Bouncy step. Well, almost

Eight p.m. Neighbors call
(disrespectful mob)
"Stop the fussing" "Here's a cake"
"Grow up, already!"

Nine p.m. Stopped the fussing
Ate the cake. But that other—
"Growing up," quite impossible
Tried so often

Eleven p.m. Reviewed the day
Scanned the decades
Searched for meanings. Found
Some sort-ofs. Gave it up

Tomorrow will be better
Birthday past, pressure off
Back-to-normal fretting
Down-to-earthish angst

Midnight hour. Time doth fly
Plump the pillow, close the eye
Sandman cometh. Beddy-bye
(. . . where's my mommy?)

Creative Nonfiction by Ruth Jesness Tweed

The Vanishing Woodpile

One of the most important features of the farm place was the woodpile. Ours was located at the edge of the woods, near the outhouse, and any family member making a trip in that direction was expected to bring a few sticks back. Thus, the wood box was seldom empty and that was important. We needed a lot of wood to heat, cook. And get the boiler going for clothes washing. A large woodpile gave the family a sense of security.

My older brother, Roy, was tall and strong—a real macho guy in his late teens. It seemed the jobs that required brawn and muscle always fell on his capable shoulders. I don't remember him grumbling about stacking wood. He took pride in building a huge woodpile—especially one particular year.

The first snow came early, before the wood was cut and stacked for winter. Our mother worried and fretted that it wouldn't get done. She needn't have worried. Roy got the job done quickly. He had a little reluctant help from a younger brother but he did most of it himself, stacking a neat pile just a little off the regular path but easily accessible. It was a very big pile and would certainly keep us supplied for the season and beyond.

Roy wanted his picture taken on top of the pile so he could remember how big it was. We still have the picture in an old family album. He is balanced on top of the pile, looking proud.

There was plenty of wood for the winter and well into spring, but as the days grew longer, the wood seemed to disappear faster than we were using it. Could someone be stealing it? Mother thought it might be so but Dad pooh-poohed the idea. Our neighbors wouldn't do such a thing and the dog would bark at strangers. It must be imagination.

No—there was no denying it. The woodpile was getting smaller by the day even though we were using less wood.

The mystery continued for a few days. Then something else happened. Even though the sun shone brightly and there was no rain, the wood was wet.

A little digging among the pieces solved the mystery and explained the original super size of the pile. My parents hadn't remembered that there was a snow pile by the edge of the grove and Roy had chosen to build on top of it. That also explained a lot of other things, like my other brother's amusement and Roy's insistence on having his picture taken "before the wood was used up."

I don't remember any more details. My mother was probably upset about having to dry the wood. She probably didn't see the humor of the situation. I do know that we never had such a large woodpile again.

Poetry by Bob Bjelkengren

Random Haiku

silently it grows
bee listens for opening
rose blossom waiting

sun warms up the pond
fog rises to start the dance
dragonfly still sleeps

Poetry by Kristin Laurel

Searching for Secrets

I left the stinking apartment
the custody battle, the lawyer
and his advice,
drove around the country, hiked hills,
picked up rocks,
concentrated on the sound of crickets.
I dove into the waters of Lake Superior
with this I'll share my clarity:
"I froze my ass off."

I was caressed like a rose
whose petals are at peak bloom,
then my summer lover dumped me.
I sat down in the woods,
dug hands into earth,
mixed my tears with the soil,
swatted at the fucking mosquitoes.
I let the wind take and toss me around,
became as weightless
as dust on a piece of toilet paper.
I searched for meaning in a flock of geese,
gazed into the brown eyes of a doe
and she stared right back at me:
"Yes, you are a mess."

I went to therapy, to Church
practiced mindfulness and Zen,
burned so much incense and sage,
I set the smoke detectors off,
woke the kids from bed;
I took them up to Harney Peak,
wearing flip-flops, and ran out of water,
hiked down the Grand Canyon
fainted in a sweat lodge,
made some new friends,
read the wise words of Jesus,
the Dalai Lama, Black Elk and Thoreau,
pedaled my bike through the streets of Minnesota
listening to loud Rock 'N' Roll and
nearly hit a bus with a bumper sticker:
"The Secret of Life is Living It."

Creative Nonfiction by Elisa Korentayer

Cooking Aliens

This winter I was abducted by an alien who loves to cook. Or perhaps I was possessed by some sort of demon Betty Crocker who takes over a human body to get her baking fix. It's also possible, say local friends, that the Minnesota winter finally got to me. I'm still not sure what happened. All I know is that in the last month I have cooked more than I've ever cooked in my entire life.

I didn't start out hating to cook. When I was young, I had a hint of precocious culinary brilliance. At the age of seven, I prepared my younger brother pancakes in shades of vibrant orange and turquoise, thanks to small vials of food coloring in our pantry. At the age of ten, I baked my first chocolate cake and worked my way through a chocolate-lovers' cookbook. When I was a teenager, I cooked gourmet meals with friends. Our most impressive gastronomic adventure occurred in late December of my senior year of high school when we crafted a complete Victorian Christmas dinner featuring a roasted goose.

My early gastronomic promise diminished when I got to college. Dining halls made me complacent. I became culinarily indolent, a food sloth. Then, living for ten years in a city with 24-hour restaurant delivery, gourmet delicatessens on every corner, and an almost non-existent kitchen accelerated the deterioration of my remaining food preparation skills. Living alone also entails the first law of bachelor cooking, namely: "Any perishable ingredients purchased in order to prepare food for one person will only be sold in amounts suitable to prepare food for entire families. This will leave copious leftover ingredients that will evolve into piles of rotting food." By the time I moved to a house with a kitchen larger than a breadbox, any cooking muscles I had ever flexed were well-atrophied.

I spent my first two years of home-ownership in a state of gridlock resistance with my kitchen. I felt drained by every bout with a pan. I dreaded opening the refrigerator door to assess my limited options. If I were less of a food lover, I might have been able to make do with crackers and the occasional slice of cheese. Unfortunately, though New York City didn't do much for my cooking, its restaurants and their culinary delights only amplified my love of food.

This winter something shifted inside of me. I found myself puttering with new ingredients and leafing through cookbooks. My refrigerator started to overflow with Tupperware containers full of leftovers. My husband came home from work expecting me to force him to cook, and instead he found gourmet meals. He put his hand on my forehead to check me for a fever. "Who are you and what did you do with my wife?" he asked.

Looking back, I can point to a few precursors for my change of heart. In October, I rehearsed and performed a show in Wisconsin. My two castmates—both men—were phenomenal cooks. Rehearsal break conversations would invariably wander toward cooking. Which variety of rosemary best enhanced the flavor of New Zealand lamb? What baking method creates the crispiest bread crust? Their discussions of specialty cookware were especially baffling to me, as these two men could wax poetic about the oddest items in their kitchens. The castmate with whom I shared a kitchen had a daily bread-baking habit, and it wasn't difficult to get used to eating fresh bread every morning.

In November, I was at an Arkansas writer's colony for one month. Right above me, there was a suite geared for cooking writers complete with a state-of-the-art test kitchen. For two weeks, a culinary herbalist named Susan cooked masterful dishes and brought care packages to her fellow writers to eat.

When I returned, I discovered a slow cooker in my cabinet and tried out a recipe for Moroccan stew I'd found in a magazine. Delicious food for such little effort? I was hooked. Soon I found myself trying more complicated recipes. My efforts did not end with the edible. The next thing I knew, I was mixing up my own environmentally-friendly cleaning products from vinegars and essential oils.

My father came for a visit from Virginia in March. He is very used to living in a house kept impeccably clean by my mother. I'm not nearly as good a cleaner, but I figured I could cook him good things to eat. I made white-chocolate cheesecake with homemade raspberry sauce. I remade my successful Moroccan stew. I prepared fresh oatmeal-coconut-chocolate-chip cookies, asparagus-leek quiche, and raspberry streusel muffins. Even I was shocked at myself. I watched my hands moving and the ingredients whipping together. I saw the oven door open and my hands putting pots in and taking them out. I was in as much shock as my husband was as each dish ended up in our bellies.

My dad had never seen me cook so much before, and said so. I explained my theory about having been abducted by a cooking alien. My dad asked if I'd be willing to lend him my cooking alien so he could bring it home and have it abduct my mother. I laughed, but found myself feeling strangely possessive of my new cooking alien, and declined to let it go.

I made a flourless hazelnut-chocolate cake on Saturday. It's now Monday, and there are only two pieces left for tonight's dessert. Tomorrow, I'm going to need to ask my cooking alien to make something new. I'm very glad that I didn't agree to give it to my father to take home.

Poetry by Betty Hartnett

Haiku 2

seven children
and two smoking adults
in the lime-green dodge

Poetry by Sister Kate Martin

Biting Cold

Imagine a great white bear with icicle teeth.
All night he growls at the wind
and prowls the frosty ground,
his cumbrous paws shaking the earth,
his breath rising like blue smoke.

By day he paces the shoreline
where the steely lake lies in its glass bowl.
His fur glimmers among the pines
as he hunts down the pale northern sunlight

And when he has seized and eaten it,
he sleeps in the shadows. Quietly
snow begins to fall.

Poetry by Susan Perala-Dewey

Reds

Kettle rattles and shakes
Steam rises
Skins split

Like my red skin seeping with sweat
Running with streams of children's chatter
Brooms batten down with dust

From the Kuusamo border of Eastern Finland
Where my relatives were whisked away
Each time believing they secured a foothold

Eyes still hold despair
Sunken, red-lined almonds
Tentative downward facing

Steam pushes
Metal clatters against pressure
By Russians, Germans, Stalin and Hitler

Second evacuation
Unexpected brutal winter
Little Ano did not survive

Cover clangs onto stovetop
Spits, spatters, eyes split
Spots of red and white

Signs of salt
Hard fought winters
Wars never quite won.

Published by the Jackpine Writers' Bloc

Poetry by Karsten Piper

The Pelicans Return to Seven Mile Lake

One pelican passes swimming
and one farther, and one farther yet.
And yet. And the infinite pelican
passes into the sun's reflection.

Does anything
glide low and parallel
like four pelicans that dream
of flight without effort?

These three arrive and splash
three interlocking water-circles.

Two pelicans coast past each other
and are for one moment one
black bird with many wings
and a gold corona.

No birds just now,
the wind remembers, though, and breathes
straight paths across the lake.

Poetry by Marilyn Heltzer

Minnesota February

I have never known how to pronounce his middle name
Percy Bysshe Shelley but I do know this about him
He never lived in Minnesota.
Because
He wrote, "If winter comes, can spring be far behind?"
And the answer is a resounding, screamed, table-pounding
     YES
Far behind.

It has been winter now since November
And I am really sick of it.
I know there are two months more at least,
March for sure and some years it snows the most in April
So Shelley you are wrong, wrong, wrong.
But of course you're dead

But we're still here, and the sun shines on the snow
And I will go now to pull on warm clothes
And Sorrel boots
And walk down the snowy township road to pick up the
     paper.
And yes,
Winter will go on. And on.
And spring, dear Percy, is far, far behind.

Poetry by Marilyn Wolff

Saturday Night Religion

He serves up
his Saturday night sermon
in tall frosty glasses
of amber brew
to his weekly customers
who file in and
religiously claim
their favorite barstool.

To the music of Hank Williams
and Johnny Cash,
they await their turn in
the confessional,
drowning their sins in a sea
of liquid oblivion.

Fiction by Jerry Mevissen

Weather

It wasn't Kate's idea to buy the tavern. But it was the only tavern Jim could afford, if he could afford this one. She had seniority at K-Mart, was thought of as management material. But Jim, her husband, he had this wild hair up his ass that some day he'd own a tavern. No thought about rookie hired help that robbed you blind, or liability insurance that cost a bundle, or a liquor license that renewed yearly at the whim of the city council. None of that.

This town at the edge of the prairie wasn't her idea either. Winter six months of the year. Snow. Naked stretches of cropland to the north that gave the arctic headwinds a free ride, pounding the tavern, sculpting snowbanks around the entry, banking the parking area. This is not where she hoped to set down her roots, to increase and multiply.

And the patrons, as motley a crew as can be rallied. A typical assembly here tonight. Kate doesn't know their names, never bothered to learn them. She calls them Weatherman, Motor Head, and Mr. Conspiracy, which is what everyone calls them. Weatherman is front and center, what with a forecast of the storm of the century threatening. Motor Head allows as how his GMC four-wheel-drive pickup will make it through damn near anything winter throws at him. Conspiracy sits alone at the end of the bar; no one is willing to listen to his current tirade against Big Pharm, which has a cure for cancer, but is keeping it under wraps.

And where is Jim tonight? Home, of course, watching the Timberwolves. He could have watched the game here at the tavern, but the regulars are not basketball fans, preferring the weather channel with its repeating maps of drifting cold fronts and dissecting isobars.

Wind rams the tavern's north wall; the lights flicker. "Doesn't look good," Weatherman says. "Could be in for a big one. Hope you got some candles," he yells to Kate.

The phone rings. "Power is out here at the house," Jim says. "Right when the Wolves were ready to rally. Likely to lose telephone lines too. Anything going on there?"

"What am I to do if the power fails?" She hears a buzz.

"Hello? Hello?"

"Doesn't sound good," says Weatherman.

"You got a generator?" asks Motor Head.

"How the hell would I know?" Kate answers.

A blast of north wind slams the door open into a waist-high drift on the stoop. Weatherman rotates off his stool and scrambles to close it. "Damn. This is serious. I should've figured we'd be in for trouble with that east wind today. It's a bad omen."

"Not to worry," says Motor Head. "I'll get everybody home."

"No one in his right mind would go out in this stuff."

Kate monitors the television. A blizzard warning for this part of the state. High winds. Drifting snow. Falling temperatures. Travel not advised. She rummages through the emergency drawer for a flashlight. She spots a first aid kit, and a billy club which she removes.

"Pour us another round, Kate," says Weatherman. "One for you and one for the Grand Conspirator, too."

Kate pours for the customers and a blackberry brandy for herself. "Has this happened before? A power failure in a blizzard?"

"Hell, yes," says Weatherman. "It happened all the time when Sully owned the bar. Mostly 'cause he didn't pay his electric bill. He kept a box of candles in the drawer with the telephone books. I expect they're still there."

Kate finds a box of votive candles and places them around the bar and one beside the cash register. "You won't need that if the power goes out," Motor Head says.

"Good old Sully," Weatherman continues. "Used to plunk the Old Crow down right here when the lights went out, and he'd take a stool right there. We'd sit out the storm, and nobody left 'til it quit or the break of dawn, whichever came first."

"That's why Sully is history," Kate says.

"That's why Sully is legend," says Weatherman.

Another blast of wind, and the sign that hangs over the stoop scrapes and scratches. "Must've snapped the guy wires," Motor Head says. "Look at that north wall. It's heavin' in those gusts. Wonder how long the old studs will take it?"

"Don't worry about us old studs," Weatherman says. "Age and cunning will trump youth and vigor any day. But I think we have a date with destiny tonight. And there's the four of us. We've got a quorum. How 'bout you, Mr. Conspirator? Wanna comment on global warming?"

"Or how about the real story that Detroit and the oil companies are covering up? That there's an engine out there good for a hundred miles a gallon," Motor Head adds.

Another gust of wind, and the door heaves open again. Kate ducks below the counter and hears someone rush to close it. The overhead lights flicker; the neons go dark. Now it's black. Kate flicks her cigarette lighter and lights candles. *Damn that Jim. Him and his big ideas. And where is he? Sitting in front of the woodstove, warm and toasty, sippin' a Baileys.*

"Well, the good news is that we're not going to die of thirst," Weatherman says.

"Do you think we're safe in here?" Kate asks.

"When your time's up, your time's up," Motor Head says. He raises his glass in a toast. "To mortality. Long may it wave."

"Put it this way," Weatherman says. "You'll last a hell of a lot longer in here than you would out there."

Kate carries a candle and walks from behind the bar to the window. Total darkness. A clatter of snow and sleet scratches the glass; a draft of frigid air chills her face. The candle flickers and dies. The aroma of hot wax transports her. Birthday cakes. Christmas dinner. Benediction at St. Mary's.

"Better get away from the window," Weatherman says.

Kate is startled, paralyzed, mute. He walks to her and leads her to a stool in front of the bar. She stares at him, stares at the other two. He rounds the corner of the bar and pours her a glass of blackberry brandy. "Drink this. It'll relax you."

She gulps and chokes and senses a familiar warmth, a pleasant sting.

"Do it again," he says.

She does, and he refills her glass. "Relax. We'll get through this."

She plants her elbows on the bar and concentrates on a faint whistle, the wind finding a chink in the building's exterior. "I'm a fish out of water," she says to no one.

She hears the door open, Motor Head rushing out, rushing back with a tool box. She hears furniture moving. The pool table and the jukebox pushed against the wall. Tables tipped on their sides, one propped against the door. Cardboard cartons opened, flattened, and tacked over the windows. She pours another blackberry brandy and stares at the huge Culligan bottle at the end of the bar, stuffed with coins and bills for the Marxon boy's surgery.

Her abbreviated K-Mart career crops up. Her colleagues, the Community College dropouts who took a job to get out of the house, away from the old man and the kids. Or to get an employee discount. People she spoke to less after a couple years than she speaks to these customers. And trusted less than that. "I don't know your names," she shouts.

"I'm Will," Weatherman answers. "That's Manny." He points his hammer toward Motor Head. "And that's Al." He points to Mr. Conspiracy.

"Aren't you married?" Her voice cracks. "Aren't you worried about your wives?" She pushes her glass forward and slouches to the bar. Her shoulders shudder; her fingers tighten around her arms. "Aren't they worried about you?"

Morning. Kate awakens to a pounding on the door, footsteps across the floor, a table moving. She is lying on seat cushions spread on the floor, covered with her coat, her pillow a couple rolls of paper toweling. Her mouth is dry, her tongue swollen and tasting of putrid berries. She raises her head to see Jim in the door, his snowmobile suit silhouetted against a lemon morning sun. The tavern is dark and disheveled, furniture stacked against walls and windows.

"Kate, where are you?" Jim pulls off his helmet.

"We made a bed for her at the end of the bar," Will says. "She damn near lost it in the storm."

Kate sits up, checks the buttons on her blouse, checks that they're buttoned in the right buttonholes.

Will watches her recover, watches her puzzlement over what may have happened. He deflects a chuckle to Manny, "I hope we didn't disappoint her."

"I know what you're thinking." Jim walks to her, his palms raised to fend off her contempt. "We'll sell this place. Move back to town. I know what you're thinking."

Kate looks at him, looks at Will, looks at Manny lying on the floor under the pool table cover, resting on an elbow, watching.

No, you don't know what I'm thinking. You don't have the slightest idea.

Note: This a member of the board of directors of the Jackpine Writers' Bloc. This work, and all work in the book by the editorial board members or board of directors of the JWB, is not eligible to go to the celebrity judges or receive prizes.

Poetry by Nicole Borg

The Box

Your first mistake is in thinking
you *want* to know what's inside.

The box has no lock,
just a simple clasp even a child could work.
Your fingers go there, as if to an old wound,
tracing a scar
or the raised tissue of an imaginary hurt.
You press your ear to the cool top,
thinking you hear the delicate scraping of wings
or the shudder of something helpless.
The truth is alive, trapped—
it is only humane to let it out.

The box is of some rich wood
polished smooth.
You see your hungry reflection there—
your eyes grown wide, your face gaunt,
your gnarled hands reaching and reaching.
You look away, hard.
It was no different with Eve—
the only fruit in the Garden
forbidden to eat.

Your second mistake is in thinking
you can resist.

Creative Nonfiction by Andy Schwaderer

The Origins of Oktoberfest

The following is a story/lecture on what we can learn and take away from a mass-brewing event, aside from a massive hangover and a town drunk.

Oktoberfest originated in the early 19th century in Munich, Germany, which was then under the rule of King Ludwig—Ludwig the Mad. Drowned by own citizens for raising taxes on beer from five pfennigs to seven. (Lesson # one: don't piss off alcoholics.) To celebrate the wedding to his, ummm, not quite lovely bride (she had a *great* personality), he ordered a festival to be held for two weeks where they would drink nothing but . . .

wine. (Lesson # two: never judge a book by its cover, or a beer festival by its, name, I guess.) That's not really a lesson, more something to think about.

Well, after a year just about everyone had recovered, aside from Ludwig who was, of course, married. Anyway, they decided to hold it again, except this time they wanted to include . . .

a trade show. Yep, thus was born our idea of a "fair." Not sure if they handed out blue ribbons to the kid who raised the fattest rabbit, but you can bet they had deep-fried Snickers, as evidenced by today's Renaissance Festivals.

Okay, so finally after two years they decided to include beer because the climate had changed in the area and it was getting too expensive coming up with the money for all that cursed French wine. (Lesson # three: do not ever, under any circumstances, depend on getting a good bottle of French wine at a decent price if you speak only English.) Ludwig had pulled a coup the first two times, and purchased the bulk of that wine on credit. Unfortunately, several months passed before he looked at the LIBOR and his variable interest rate, and decided he needed more income.

He attempted raising the taxes, but was quick to notice the pitchforks and burning torches thrusting in through his window by the unhappy base of the party. So, Ludwig relented, repealed the tax, and called on the good monks of the area to begin brewing beer in massive quantities. Now, they had been performing miracles and brewing beer for centuries and so they had the chops to provide the quantity, but they also threatened to drink up all his profits. To, ummm, properly motivate them, Ludwig decreed that no monk could drink more than six liters of beer in one day, which of course was just one of the "miracles" they performed daily.

Okay, time out from the lesson plan to focus on that. That's insane. That's a gallon and a half of beer, and we're not talking Lite Schlitz here. This is heavy, brooding, German beer. This is the land of Freud, and perhaps that's also why the beer can be personality-altering. Anyway, back to the story . . . . Well, the monks said "Okay" and weaned themselves—over months—down to only six liters of beer a day. The increase in sexual prowess was no doubt moot, but maybe they lived longer or something else of some partial value.

Regardless, the modern day beer garden was born, or should I say brewed. It perhaps is most fitting that Bayer aspirin was created in the same region as this beer festival; proof that necessity is the mother of all invention.

Editor's Choice Poetry by Timothy Otte

Minneapolis Winter, '05

It's nights like tonight you earn
that shot of schnapps in your hot cocoa.

By the time you've shoveled the snow
from one end of the walk to the other
you almost have to shovel your way back.

It's better to simply convince yourself
you've made a dent in it, trudge back inside
stomp your boots on the mat inside the door,
hang your coat up, shake off the snow.

Your hair is less gray with snowflakes in it.

Throw the dog his bone, pour that shot into your mug,
sit down to catch the ten o'clock news.

Later you'll fall asleep alone.

Published by the Jackpine Writers' Bloc

Poetry by Marsh Muirhead

thumbs

among these
oaks
above
these streets
at the
democratic
speed of light
little feet
of
words
the twitter
patter
of
tiny
speak

Creative Nonfiction by Beverly A. Erickson

Sweet Dairy Queen Memories

"Welcome to the Dairy Queen. May I help you?" My face flushed as I greeted customers. I was fourteen, puny, and shy as a mouse.

Torn between shyness and a burning desire to earn money to buy a clarinet so I could join the high school band, I applied for a job at my small hometown Dairy Queen. Home alone my first day of summer vacation, the phone rang, startling me.

"Hello," I answered.

On the other end, I heard a voice begin rumbling like the worn out muffler on my Mom's old Chevy. "This is Barken, owner of the Dairy Queen. My going rate is thirty-five cents an hour. I'll hire you on a three week trial. You meet my standards—you keep the job. You don't—you're fired. Training's at eight tomorrow morning."

"Thanks, Mr. Barken," I politely responded. "I'll be there."

Hanging up the phone, my knees trembled. My mind raced. *Mr. Barken sounds mean; what if I don't meet his standard? I need money; it has to be better than babysitting; I hope my friends stop at the DQ.*

The next morning, chills iced my spine as I stepped inside the back door of the Dairy Queen. The air-conditioned interior, humming stainless steel machines, finely brushed stainless counter tops and a disinfectant smell reminded me of a hospital.

"You're on time!" Mr. Barken said, surprised. "We'll work on cones. Once you learn to make cones, the rest is uphill."

Hovering like a gruff giant, Mr. Barken instructed me on the standards of making a five-ounce cone. Oozing from the open spigot of the refrigerated ice cream dispenser, a smooth white rope of soft-serve crème filled the cone in my hand. Swiftly twisting my wrist, I swirled a curl onto the top of the crème and shut off the spigot.

Over and over, Mr. Barken repeated, "Dump it out. Dump it

out. Do it until you get it right."

I dumped mounds of soft crème until, at last, I created the perfect curly-topped cone, registering five ounces on the counter scale. I met his standards. With half a smile, Mr. Barken said, "You're a keeper."

As I had hoped, over the following weeks, friends did stop and order sweet vanilla DQ treats topped with mouth-watering chocolate, strawberries, bananas, and other delights. A cute boy with steely blue eyes stopped each day and ordered a Jack and Jill Sundae. He said the way the hot fudge melted the ice cream and marshmallow topping, it looked like a lava flow.

Over the next three summers, I served thousands of taste-tantalizing DQ treats. "Music to my ears," Mr. Barken would say, hearing the *kaa-ching* of the cash register, as I deposited the customer's money.

My boss learned to like me. I really liked the blue-eyed boy. And, I learned to play my clarinet well. After graduation, I went to college, became a nurse, and married that cute boy.

My hometown Dairy Queen turned out to be a real sweet place to work.

Poetry by Brianna Lynne Fynboh *(age: 16)*

Plucking Flower Petals: An Acrostic

A lovely, warm,
Nervous feeling in the
Tips of my fingers and toes,
Isolating the most
Curiously vulnerable parts
In my typically independent, not-so-
Patient nature. It isn't just
Another wishful dream.
This time, you're real, and
I'm real, and
Only the clinging insecurity threatens the
Nerves I once had so carefully wrapped in iron . . . .

Published by the Jackpine Writers' Bloc

Poetry by Nancy Bachhuber Massman

Sound of Silence

The sound of silence fills the neighborhoods
Games are stilled, talk suspended
Traffic done for the day.

Yet, I hear
deep inside I hear the memories
a waltz plays in my head
my toes keep time
children laugh
birds chirp and sing.
I hear a breeze tease my skin
a distant dove mourns.

Beethoven was deaf
but he heard the music.

Honorable Mention Creative Nonfiction
by Betty Hartnett

The Ride Home

It had been a long day. That night, after singing in the choral concert, I wanted only to get home; that was all that was on my mind. I had made arrangements for staying the night with my friend, Mary, but she must have forgotten. The doors were locked, and I knocked on both doors for some time. But she wasn't home.

Then I went to Anderson Hall, the nearest dorm, to ask if they had a guest room available for the night, but they were all taken.

I was exhausted. We had practiced for the fall concert, my first at the U. of M., all morning and then sang two concerts in the evening. I was dreading taking the city bus to St. Paul Park and then calling my dad. It would be past midnight. He had said to call when I needed a ride. Sure, he would come and get me, but I was eighteen, and shouldn't have to have my dad pick me up. If only Mary had been home.

As I walked down Washington Avenue toward the bus stop, two young guys pulled up alongside the street.

"Hey, where you going?" one of them asked in a friendly voice. "Need a ride?"

I judged them to be about my age, eighteen or so. I felt no fear. Their radio was blaring "Chances Are," my favorite Johnny Mathis tune, and their beat-up Chevy jalopy looked harmless. All the kids had beaters in those days, if they had a car at all.

"To the bus stop," I said. "I'm going home."

"Where's that?" he asked.

"Oh, it's a long way from here. I'm going to take the bus and then my dad will pick me up."

"Why don't you hop in? We'll give you a ride home."

"No. Thanks. It's too far."

"We don't have anything to do anyway. Doesn't matter how far it is."

"No, really, it's too far, almost an hour away. The bus will be fine."

"Heck, we're going to be up all night driving around. Nothing's going on around here. It's not a problem."

I couldn't believe what he was saying. That would be so terrific. My fatigue had definitely blocked my reasoning and judgment. I still entertained no fear. (To this day, my lack of concern baffles me.) I was quite sure they weren't University students. Maybe it was the way they spoke. Also, no students I knew drove around all night. But they seemed nice. Some of my friends weren't going to college either.

I then said, "Okay, if you're sure it's not too much trouble."

"Nope, it'll be fine," he said, and he hopped out of the car. He took my suitcase and bag of concert clothes and put them in the back seat. He closed the back door and motioned for me to sit in the middle of the front seat.

I got in, feeling for the first time a little uncertain and somewhat awkward sitting between two strangers. The other guy, the driver, said, "Hi," and then was silent. As Johnny Mathis was still singing "Chances Are," we began to talk a little about him, and I remember laughing about something, though I don't remember what it was.

Then the driver asked if I'd like a Coke. He said there was an A&W close by. I said that was fine, if it wasn't very far, because I wanted to get home as quickly as I could. I was tired.

We drove to the drive-in and bought Cokes. After sitting and drinking for about five minutes, they were ready to go. I noticed that the driver was now very quiet, and possibly annoyed at something. The atmosphere had changed and had become tense.

Suddenly, I realized we were on an isolated, wooded road. I said, "Hey, where are we going?" The car stopped and the driver got out, slamming the door.

"What do you mean, where are we going?" the remaining guy said. "We're here, just you and me." He began to grab at my clothes.

"What are you doing?" I yelled.

He didn't reply, but continued to rip my blouse. I was

frightened now. I tried to move over and push him away, but he blocked my hands and arms with his left arm and shoulder. With his right hand, he reached to the back of my skirt and tried to tear it open. Failing that, he thrust his hand under my skirt. I was wearing a full length Maidenform panty girdle. Thank God for girdles! For the next several minutes, he struggled to take off my girdle. My hands were pinned, so I could do nothing but twist my body to make his task more difficult. Finally, I said, "Please, mister."

"Mister?" he said, as if he was shocked. At that moment, I realized that he probably was sixteen or seventeen, younger than I. His determination had definitely waned with his failure with my girdle and, after I had spoken, he stopped. I could tell he was upset and angry. He got out of the car and flung the door shut.

Almost immediately, the driver reappeared. I hadn't had time to think to lock the doors. I moved to the opposite door. My blouse was ripped but everything else, though out of place, was okay.

As he got into the car, he said, "I'm going to take you home." He sounded like he meant what he said. I didn't want to get out of the car because the other guy might be near.

Then he said, "I didn't want him to do what he did." Now I was confused. I didn't know if I should believe him, but what other choice did I have?

We drove home, talking occasionally. I remember nothing about our conversation. When we finally arrived at my house, he walked me to the door, apologized again, and left. I may have thanked him. I don't remember.

Poetry by Marsh Muirhead

Construction

I tap the brake, crack the window,
drum my fingers on the steering wheel,
scan the radio for something mellow,
check my memory for what it was
I couldn't be late for, what time, what place
was being robbed by barricades and cones,
the flashing lights of a construction zone,
ruts and piles of dirt, the road scarred,
disappearing in the chaos and the rain.

Such inconvenience this detour from the day,
halted by giant yellow dragons belching black
exhaust, time lost in moving dirt and rock, the
thick-armed captains riding high, wheeling,
dipping, bouncing towards the sky, carving out
other directions, the roads of other travelers.

Stopped by a flag, I take an off ramp to the past,
descend toward roads and cities in a sandbox.
I am blading, hauling, moving earth,
turning over the heavy sand with a grader—
my palm, the sand rolling over, cool, dark,
any shape I want—hills, valleys, villages,
nothing lost, no cost, roads and racetracks,
mountains or a fortress, any whim granted,
anything a king or a kingdom might invent.

Poetry by Gwen Schock Cowherd

Perfect Words

My teacher said to write a poem.
The perfect words will come.
You'll see.
I drive the lonely prairie road
searching for rhythm and rhyme.
Most words I choose are too simple;
they stutter, don't flow.
Prairie wind blows my perfect words away.
Fields of golden wheat stalks
lean close, whisper, bend, and pivot
as wind directs mating dances.
Wheat's fertile sensual grain heads
listen for wind's perfect words
before casting seeds for nature's
rhythm and rhyme.

Poetry by Anne M. Dunn

Crone Song

We crones have gone beyond
The call of our own voice of innocence
And with our hand upon the door
We stand looking into another world
To which we do too soon depart.

Our blood will feed the giddy worms,
Our flesh enrich the soil.
Perhaps the roots of a maple
Will clutch my rigid bones.
Then those who tap the tree
Will get a taste of me
And wonder at such sweetness.

Or will a heron flying home at dusk
Listen as an owl perched in my strong limbs
Mutters a message to the future?

Or will I rise from the grave
A graceful blue violet
To be praised with the simple joy
Of a wandering butterfly?

Or shall I find my rest
On a bed of moss where a shy child
Will press her eager ear
Against my velvet mouth to hear
My songs of awe full love?

Poetry by Susan McMillan

Anthology

This day, a poem!
The hoarfrost glistening white,
edges of every limb and weed
softened by beards of lace.

Skeletons of dead summer parsnip blossoms
now bursting fireworks, silver plumes
against needly curtains of blackest spruce
decked out in wintertime garb.

This life, *The Collected Works!*
Anthology of poem-days,
three-hundred-sixty-five various themes
times fifty-four years and counting.
How many is that? How many days

of rubber-soled kid's shoe scraping, climbing
limbs of old apple trees, snowy in bloom,
knees bent, upside-down hanging,
fingertips brushing spiky grass
dripping green, the world bottom-up?

How many nights wading fallow fields,
tall, soppy grass heads slapping bare calves
while fog gathers slow and cool with the twilight,
rising in blankets of spiderweb film?

How many walks on the rocky shore,
bare feet bruised and blue with cold,
Gitche Gumee grumbling away
in ancient and rattly voice from the deep,
his fresh breath strong from the north?

How many more strides of this body of mine,
the kick and glide of my skis
singing the only song in this snow
along freshly-groomed trails (bless someone for that!)
where I move between river and trees?

Each moment a stanza punctuated by glint
of glittering diamonds haphazardly strewn . . .
with the rabbit's tracks, I gather them up
and tomorrow, write them all down!

Creative Nonfiction by Hope Klocker

Some People's Faults

It was the end of summer; we were driving back from Fandel's department store with bags of new school clothes for me piled in the back seat. Once a year, my mother, Honey, would take only me to town to shop for school clothes. My younger sisters would cry and beg to go with but, for once, my mother ignored them. Of course, I savored these rare moments alone with her since I knew this was pretty much it for a whole year. She seemed happy and relaxed and not the least bit worried about the cost of things I'd picked out. The day was shaping up to be the highlight of this particular summer.

On the way home, we rolled into the gas station in our small town and waited for the attendant to come out. Honey tapped her finger on the steering wheel and stared straight ahead, which alerted me to trouble. I turned my head to look, knowing whatever it was it was coming our way. I watched as the owner, Mr. J., ambled toward us, dipping his head to check out who was behind the wheel.

"Fill her up?" he said, giving my mother a wink. Honey nodded without looking at him, still tapping her finger. Mr. J. gave me one of his charming-guy winks and I smiled but quickly looked away, embarrassed that such a rich man would even notice me. He cranked the handle on the gas pump, hauled the hose around the car, and stuffed it in the tank. In those days, the attendant always washed the windshield and checked the oil. Mr. J. spent a lot of extra time washing the window in front of my mother, whistling and grinning.

After he swabbed the wiper blades and snapped them back in place, he leaned into my mother's open window. "Saw Dirk last night," he said smiling. "Yup, he was staggering down the street."

Honey stared straight ahead like she didn't hear him.

"I saw him fall down too, right in the gutter."

Mr. J. waited for Honey to say something, but her lips were

sealed. "Katie, Katie, how'd a good-looking girl like you end up with a guy like that?"

I thought I was going to die of embarrassment and, what was worse, I knew that every kid at school would hear about my drunk dad and tease me to tears. I watched my mother reach into her purse and pull out her wallet. She didn't look like she'd heard what Mr. J. had said but I could tell she was going to say something now and it made my heart race so fast I could hear it. She gave him some money and then, after a year-long minute, she turned to face him.

"J. . . ." she said in the sweetest, calmest voice I'd ever heard her speak, "J., the way I see it, some people's faults are just more obvious than others."

Then she put that new Buick in gear and we sailed on home.

Poetry by Betty Hartnett

Haiku 1

midst conversation
the word I wanted
took flight

Poetry by Penelope Swan

First Child: The Story She Tells/Retells

is I'm the one who did not want
to cuddle or rock. Or arrange my head
on shoulder and fall into restful hours
of sleep in clasped curve of warmth
my baby breath on her neck
assurance I was alive.

                  Instead I knocked myself out
held up my head
dug in tiny toes to climb high
to peer into the beyond behind her.

You are the only one she says
who'd wrestle out of my arms
strain to stand on my lap
and look out
at the world. It hurt my thighs.

                  Do I wish I had risen with ease
                      to her motherly heart's dream?

This—yet another retelling is an arraignment;
why even strangers are nodding in sympathy.
Her ending doesn't change: *Too independent, this one.*

Sorry says I. Remember I inherited sturdy legs and walked
    early.

Poetry by Deborah A. Davis

the game of crumbs

if i don't eat today
my father will actually have loved me

famish

so she plays the games of crumbs
one crumb, two crumbs make a meal

wait

but memories stick in her throat
like the bits she needs to live

purge

life pouring out, not in
expunging, flushing all the sin

repeat

Fiction by Tarah L. Wolff

Browsing

When Elizabeth was her own daughter's age, her mother would set her on a hip and twirl her around the kitchen. They would turn up the jade green radio on the counter all the way. Her mother's long tanned legs would toss her skirt and her shining black hair would fly. Supper would be cooking and they would dance before her father got home.

Wal-Mart was quiet this late at night. She wandered the aisles, her flip-flops *skif, skif, skiffing* along the smooth floors. She opened the music boxes, considered buying one for her daughter. The ballerinas stood poised with long legs and arms stretched out around beautiful, smiling faces. She lingered, touching the ballerina's bright face. Her hair was blond but she really did look like her mother used to look, when she still danced, when she was still young. Her mother still had that little jade radio; she had no idea why she would ever have kept it. She never would have.
She shut the music box and left it on the shelf.

It was the angry-trying-to-be-quiet that always woke her. At night, after they put her to bed, the violence in the air would become a thick, inescapable entity. Her mother was his victim. Listening to the beating, she would lay there waiting for him to come for her. She saw him coming through her door, standing over her bed and reaching with his black fingers. But he never touched her and her mother's bruises were always well-covered in the morning.

She made her way to grocery. Picked up boxes of macaroni and cheese and cat food. She wandered down frozen food and eyed the ice cream through the glass. The reflection of her pudgy face was blotchy and sunburned. She grabbed a gallon of chocolate and hurried away.

In fruit, she reached out and stroked the fuzzy skin of a peach. "Elizabeth?"

She froze and stared.

The old man grinned at her from beside the apples. There were two teeth missing in his smile and his thin hair was frazzled where it had been stubbornly brushed back. The plaid shirt on him was too long and hung like a raincoat.

He said, "Elizabeth? Hey! How are you?"

She clutched her cart between them. His arms lifted toward her before he pulled them back and hugged himself. He shook with the effort and he looked, embarrassed, at his feet.

She said, "I'm fine."

Her father had pushed her mother through the picture window in the front room, scattering the robins and shattering the bird bath. The impact broke her mother's back in three places, leaving her paralyzed from the waist down. Elizabeth had been in the backyard playing when she had heard the glass break. She had been eight years old and she had just hoped that her mother wasn't dead.

He leaned toward her desperately. "Your daughter. Shannon. How is she?"

Her mouth fell open. "How do you know about her?"

"Your mom wrote. Told me all about her. Sent me a picture of her." He scrambled out his thin wallet. There was nothing in it except a new driver's license and two one dollar bills. They were dirty. From behind the bills, he pulled her daughter's picture. Three years old and touch-worn to the extent that all the edges were frayed.

He stuttered, "She . . . . She's beautiful! She looks like you."

She wanted to snatch the picture out of his hand.

His dark eyes were red rimmed and wet. "She isn't here with you?"

She said, "No."

Her father had been incarcerated for twenty years. After several surgeries on her mother's body, they were given a small but new home to start again in. Just the two of them. At night, they would make dinner with the radio turned up high.

Her mother would urge her, "Dance! Dance!"

And she would try to dance the way she had seen her mother dance, with her eyes closed and her arms out. Sometimes at night, she would wake up and listen and hold her breath and wait for him. But, day after day, he was gone. And her mother would swing her arms above her head, hands waving out the beat, dancing the only way she could.

He said, "You look really good, Elizabeth. Do you have a nice place to live now?"

She thought of the crappy rental house they had last lived together in as a family.

Was struck at how long that had been now.

Over two decades.

She stuck out her chin. "I bought a house."

His eyes lit up. "That's great! Your mother told me you were thinking about that."

He reached out and stroked the fuzzy skin of a peach. It was the same peach she had touched.

"I better get going." She headed her cart toward the checkout.

He said, trying not to be too loud but he was, "It was nice to see you! I'll see you later then."

She got to the checkout, pushed her groceries up on the counter, and hurried into her purse. She had eighty-three dollars in her wallet. Behind the bills, she saw the picture she hadn't realized she had still been carrying around. Her father holding her high up as a toddler. They were both smiling. They had the same eyes.

She noticed the Wal-Mart gift cards.

She looked back at him.

Her father's bent back made him a crooked shape, an unbelievable version of the man he used to be. He was staring at the peaches as if they were about to start talking to him, or that he wished that they would.

The cashier had rung up her groceries and was looking at her expectantly.

She bit her lip. "Could you do something for me?"

The cashier raised her eyebrows at her. "What?"

"If I buy a gift card for that man, could you go give it to him?"

She pointed at him as he headed up the center aisle, wanderingly, hands in his pockets. The sole of his left shoe was flapping.

The cashier eyed the old man, then nodded. "Sure."

She put all of her cash on the gift card.

She held it for a split second before leaving it behind.

Fiction by Kristin F. Johnson

The Following Day

The funeral procession went slowly down Main Street. I was used to watching parades and happy times on that street, like celebrating the Fourth of July or when several of the boys from town had gone off to Iraq. Those times were loud with people jumping up and down and clapping and cheering from the curbs. This was quiet and still with the spectators solemn and sad. A man across the street had his little girl high up on his shoulders. He held onto her saddle shoes. She wore a lacy white dress and had pigtails tied with pink bows and probably couldn't even talk yet. She waved a tiny American flag and clapped her hands but didn't make any noise.

Mom wanted me to go even though I didn't know David Ingebretson or his family, except for seeing them at church on Sundays. "It's important for the town," she had said. "It's important for the healing."

A line of cars came through real slow, and they all had their lights on. First, there was a long black hearse that looked like it had just been washed because the sun glinted off the hood. The car that followed had David's mom and daddy in it. They didn't look out at us. They just stared straight ahead. A few other cars followed.

Soldiers marched after the cars. One line of soldiers carried rifles leaning against their shoulders. They walked all stiff like they were toy soldiers with wooden arms and legs. There were more men in uniform than I had ever seen at once in my small town. Most of the older men in Amery were veterans of this war or that one. They had all put their uniforms on for the occasion. I even saw Mr. Swenson. He looked so different out of his white grocery apron. Now he had a bunch of medals pinned to his uniform. Some of the older men, including Mr. Swenson, had bellies that made the fabric pull tight on their jackets, tighter than it maybe had been when the uniforms were new and the men were younger.

Once the procession passed through Main Street, the crowds quietly split up and my folks and I went to the truck.

The graveyard was just outside of town. Daddy didn't play the radio the whole way and no one talked. We just jiggled along on that bumpy road. Daddy parked the truck a little ways away and we walked over to where everyone was headed up the hill. The grass looked droopy and smelled dry like it needed watering.

There were flowers standing up on five tripods like the holders my teachers used in school for huge flippable pads of paper. The flowers smelled sweet in the summer air. The roses were the strongest: the scent of sadness. I didn't know the names of the other flowers. The sun was warm on my face.

The casket sat up on a platform. An American flag was draped over it, nearly covering the whole casket, except the ends and the bottom of each side. There was a deep rectangle dug into the grass and a huge mound of dirt next to it. The dirt smell was strong too, like a garden or wet dirt after a rainstorm when worms tunneled through it. I wanted to look in the hole but was afraid to, like I might fall in and get stuck. My heart pounded a little.

A chair was set out for David's mom who was all dressed in black. She had a veil over her face, probably to hide the crying. I always hated people seeing me cry, like when I went to the movies and something sad happened or even something happy that struck me so deep that the tears just spilled out.

Mrs. Ingebretson's husband stood behind her and put his hands on her shoulders. He was wearing a uniform too. Mrs. Ingebretson put her hand up to her face, under the veil. She clutched a tissue and dabbed her eyes.

A line of seven soldiers with rifles stepped forward and aimed at the sky.

One yelled, "Fire."

They shot their rifles into the air in unison. *Bamm.*

"Fire!"

Bamm.

"Fire!"

Bamm.

Smoke swirled from their gun barrels up into the clear sky and hung there. The gunpowder was sweet like the roses, or blood. They stepped back together and away from the casket.

Another soldier came forward. It was Mr. Swenson. He had a trumpet and stopped at the end of the casket. He raised the trumpet and took a deep breath.

Daddy said the song he was playing was called "Taps."

When Mr. Swenson played "Taps"on that trumpet, that's when I started crying. The sun heated the tears on my face. They ran like a faucet you couldn't turn off. The song was sad and beautiful all at once, like a honeycomb dripping and held up to the sun. But it was also so alone-feeling, like the way David was in that casket heading for Heaven and how his mom maybe felt now with him gone.

Mr. Swenson finished playing, and the last note hung in the air. He waited a second or two, then lowered his trumpet and held it straight up and down in front of him. He turned like the other soldiers had and stepped away from the casket.

Two other soldiers marched in front of Mrs. Ingebretson. Then they turned in perfect ninety-degree angles and marched over to the casket. The soldiers lifted the flag up carefully and folded it in half once lengthwise and then again until it was a skinnier strip, about a foot wide. Then one soldier folded it in a triangle again and again and again toward one end until only the blue background with the white stars was showing. Daddy had said there is a specific way of handling the American flag. You could never let a flag touch the ground or it was considered disrespectful. The way they folded that flag was perfect. It ended in a triangle, kind of like the ones we would make out of paper at school and use to play football at our table in the lunchroom, but we didn't have to be careful about how the colors were folded because the paper was all white. And paper footballs often fall on the floor.

One of the soldiers marched the folded flag over to David's mom and handed it to her. His white-gloved hand was on top of the flag as he presented it. She took it and then he saluted her. Mrs. Ingebretson held that flag to her chest with both of her hands on it, like she was holding her son. But her son was gone. She stared stone-faced at nothing in front of her. She had probably imagined her son's homecoming from the war with a huge WELCOME HOME banner over their front door and a big cake with vanilla frosting and gobs of people all smiling and hugging. Now when she wanted to talk with David, all she would have was a folded flag and a gravesite to visit.

I looked up at Mom. She was wiping a tear off her face, so I squeezed her hand to remind her I was still here. She looked down at me and smiled, a little.

Published by the Jackpine Writers' Bloc

Poetry by Harriet Duerre

The Summer Kitchen

A blizzard of feathers
Fills the old summer kitchen.
The women pluck the geese clean,
Pimpled, headless bodies cradled in their laps.

They gossip about the lazy wife on the next farm,
Dip the naked bodies into boiling pots,
Scrape pinfeathers, clip wingtips.
Steam rises and blurs their wrinkled eyes.

These old women stayed on the farm,
Milked cows, tended gardens, canned tomatoes
Fed hungry threshing crews,
Raised strapping sons and frugal daughters.

Now the farm wives go to town,
Work in factories, open a shop.
More promise and reward in that,
Than a few dollars for egg money.

The summer kitchen holds ghosts
Of the homesick, lonely ones that came first,
Their lives buried under grinding work,
Goose feathers drifting over their dreams.

Poetry by Luke Anderson

Barn Cats

Milking time draws cats of all ilk.
Toms, moms, kittens, and strays
come running to lap warm milk.
Furry heads bob around the tray
'til each has reached their fill.

Sated cats wipe their faces
with tongue-wetted paw.
Some bask in sunny places,
others climb into the hay mow.
Kittens pounce and chase.

The clan swells every year.
Twenty arrive at the meal.
Feline leukemia appears.
Many cats die in the ordeal,
but old mom cat perseveres.

Alone she arrives at the tray,
even when the winter is bitter.
Then, one sunny spring day
she brings a new litter
and the cycle replays . . . .

Honorable Mention Poetry by Doris Lueth Stengel

Vernon's White Onions

The rows of white onions
in my brother's garden
grew straight as virtue,
untainted by the gossip
of a single weed.

On my cutting board
they spill juicy little secrets
held inside all summer,
unaware they are the last onions
to be planted by his hands,
graced by his tender care.

I weep, not for onions,
but for my brother
now neatly planted in his own plot.

I chop this sweet harvest,
scoop its goodness into a stew
made from our mother's recipe.
It simmers in a cast iron pot
inherited from grandmother;
she long dead, mother long dead.
My brother's death only a rumor
until my onion bin is bare.

Creative Nonfiction by Linda M. Johnson

I Bake Bread

On the anniversary of mom's death, the date occurs to me as I assemble the ingredients to bake bread. I miss her, will always miss her, but I'm not sad. I don't think she'd want me to be. Although our time together was brief, there was a lot of love.

October sunshine spills through kitchen windows, leaves golden puddles on the counter. The dog is sprawled out on the living room floor, my husband and two sons are out running errands. After I pour myself a cup of strong, black coffee, I can't help but stop to reflect on my roots. In my quiet house it's a reverent moment. I clasp hands around the steaming mug like a prayer.

On the counter is Grandma's bread bowl. It's a large, pale yellow bowl with Ovenware USA engraved on the bottom. The top, outer edge boasts a wide maroon band, which itself has a narrow band of light blue both above and beneath it. There are tiny, spidery veins in the glazing, but there are no chips or cracks in the bowl itself. I have no clue how old it is but I love the fact I'm using something that had been Grandma's.

After my mom died when I was eight years old, I spent many hours at her mother's house. Grandma and I shared a bond. Without saying the words, I'm sure we brought each other comfort, something I didn't realize until I was an adult.

When I was at Grandma's, we spent a lot of time in her tiny kitchen, undoubtedly the heart of her home. That's where we drank coffee, read, and worked on word puzzles. It's also where we talked, which was so much more than hearing the latest on the relatives or complaining about the weather. We shared our hopes and dreams out loud while sitting at the table overlooking the backyard.

We also bumped hips working together in that small space. When we baked, I could help measure and mix, but when it came to clean-up Grandma always hand-washed the antique bowl herself. I never washed the bowl until it became mine after she passed away.

The recipe I'm using today is from my aunt on my dad's side of the family. During my dad's brief battle with cancer, my siblings and I opted to take care of him at home with the help of hospice. Living in a small community meant we knew almost everybody. Because so many people came to visit Dad during his final weeks, I think of that time as a living wake. My aunt came faithfully, every single day. Dad was the youngest in his family and because she was one of the oldest in their large farming family, to her he was always her "baby" brother.

And so it was not long after Dad died, my aunt and I spent a day together, connected by the need to be with someone else who loved the man we both mourned. My aunt came over to teach me how to make biscuit, that sweet, cardamom-infused bread, a staple in Finnish homes.

So many memories are made in a kitchen; so much in our lives revolves around the spiritual unity of family and food.

Today I grind cardamom seeds in my coffee grinder. The aromatic scent of the seeds is love itself; I breathe in deep, imagine the pungent fragrance spiraling straight to heaven.

While I'm wrist-deep kneading dough, my thoughts are still on family. My nephew has asked me to teach him how to make biscuit. I vow to call him next time I decide to bake. My sister has a grandchild now and it occurs to me I should have her bring him over so he can taste his heritage. By the time my boys get home later today, the biscuit will just be coming out of the oven. I know they'll cut into a loaf immediately; their favorite way to embrace their Finnish roots is their love of cardamom bread.

There is no denying the ingredients of my past formed me, made me who I am. Today, I shape loaves, watch my future rising before me.

Poetry by Roberta Tietge

Clocking Out

It's days like this when I come home from work
and wish I were my cat Jimmy,
whose champion challenge lies in
pursuing the patch of sun
as it slowly slips across the floor.

My fiercest adversary would be the young feline
that lives in the same house,
who's outgrown me.

Still, I would reap sweet satisfaction
in rabbit-kicking the spry one about the chin,
sending him, tail swishing madly,
to groom himself, trying to garner some dignity
after a thorough thrashing.

Poetry by Tara McDaniel

The Treatment

My grandmother, there in the hallway,
didn't cry, didn't wring her hands or sigh,
though my mother was groping her
though she wouldn't stop repeating
Please.

Instead, she grabbed my mother
by the thick of her arms and shook her
once, twice, then once more. She said,
Stop it, Sam. Stay in your room!

It may sound cold now, but the reasons then
were of course simple:
My mother was diagnosed. She was alone.
My grandmother left her new husband
so she could care for her daughter
and for me, too.

After that, my grandmother made me breakfast
for dinner: bacon drip
over white flour biscuits and eggs
with the bacon cut up in them, and the jar
on the table sticky with blackberry jam.

She smiled and patted my arm
a lot.

For the next couple days I didn't see my mother:
she wouldn't come out of her room.
Grandmother dozed at the kitchen counter,
propped up sideways on her elbow.
It was like the hand that cupped her face
tilted her ear just towards the hallway,
in case there was the tiniest noise, or the littlest reason to be
a young mother again, to rush into that room . . .
her hand a cool respite against the fevered bloom.

Fiction by Susan Koefod

Bare Hands

A woman in her early seventies arrives at the bus stop, smiles, and notes the coldness of the weather. She compliments you on your very warm-looking coat. Her hair is softly waved; she's wearing antique pearl earrings, and her complexion is delicate and smooth, despite her age. Her own coat is conservative, unflattering and modest, the kind of coat you remember your own mother wearing to church.

She immediately tells you about the mothers she's seen waiting with their children for the bus, oh they have their children all bundled up, but the mothers aren't wearing any gloves. How terrible it is, all of those mothers with bare hands. She shivers for them. You see her glancing at your hands, but they are buried deep in your pockets.

For once, you find yourself face to face with a simple graceful conversation about nothing at all—the weather, the uncovered hands of mothers out in the cold—a small decency that one does not have to spend any time weighing for significance (what a relief that is). How you've longed for such a simple moment. For a little scene that wouldn't dream of starring in the story of your day.

And—it has all the flavor of a used tea bag at the bottom of your empty cup. Still, you tell yourself to enjoy it. Enjoy the moment. Isn't it what you wanted? Something completely ordinary? For once?

You shove your hands deeper in your pockets and walk away from her. The last thing you want is to engage in conversation with a stranger who will be in your life for maybe all of ten minutes. This, you remind yourself, is why you never take the bus anymore. It was silly to think that today's spur of the moment trip would make any difference in the life you've settled into. You begin to ask yourself, as you knew you would, why did you bother? This little "escape" you called it, an afternoon away from work, away from the house, away from any responsibilities. You're not sure where you are going, really, you're never sure where you are going. You left the house without any real purpose. But that was the point, wasn't it? And now your hands are starting to get cold. You long to pull them out of your pockets, rub them together, and blow on them, but then you'd be exposed. And you aren't sure you want, or deserve, her pity.

At last, the bus arrives and you are surprised to hear yourself telling her—"The bus is coming." She thanks you with genuine courtesy that manages to make you cringe. You let her get on the bus before you and she drops a few quarters, the senior citizen rate, into the till. Your cold hands fumble with your dollars; you are not really sure what the fare is. You manage to feed a few dollars in and make your way to a seat. She sits near the front and you find a spot a few rows back.

More passengers board every few blocks. The older woman seems to know them all, bestows on all of them that same generous smile and greeting. She chats with them about other people they apparently know in common though, for all you know, the other riders are perhaps just being polite (more polite than you were) and pretending to know what she is talking about.

The bus continues on its way, turns to follow the river bluff, and then in a few blocks, she signals and stands up. The bus stops and the bus driver asks her to wait, he'll pull ahead to a clearer spot, though she says it really isn't necessary. He still does it anyway and when she steps down, she says "Thank you," to the bus driver. Everyone watches as she enters a small café where, you expect, she will greet everyone warmly inside and they will bring her the same cup of soup she orders every Monday.

Now that she's gone, you miss her. You knew you would. You almost wish you'd gotten off the bus, too, and gone inside the restaurant with her. You might have ordered the same soup she's having, that homey chicken vegetable soup they make that really comes from a can, but she doesn't care, it's fine with her, she wouldn't even dream of pointing out that it's the same old soup she buys from the grocery store. She will sit in her usual spot by the cashier, sipping her soup, mentioning the cold weather, telling of the mothers without gloves, cupping her hands around her coffee cup to warm them.

The bus drives on, carrying you away with your obsessive thoughts that are so desperately trying to collect themselves into a purpose you call today.

Poetry by Virginia Miller

The 100th Birthday

Time is no longer her enemy
she no longer needs to be right
A smile and a nod will do
remembering the past is joy

The world is on its own
younger people's responsibility

Honorable Mention Poetry by Candace Simar

Alzheimer's, Early Onset

The first twinge of confusion barely blipped the radar. He was stressed, needed a vacation. So what if he lost his way? He bought some vitamins, had a physical. It was nothing a few days off wouldn't cure.

He felt better after the Bahamas, tanned and rested. But he quit giving power-point presentations after he forgot what he was talking about in mid-sentence during an important meeting. He covered well, made a joke, and changed the format to a Q&A session instead. No one guessed the missing pieces of memory. No one saw the black holes eating his brain.

He adapted. Made a big push to give the associates a larger role in the company. He was fifty-five. Time to step back a little and groom his future replacements.

His wife insisted he see a specialist after she spotted the Post-it note stuck on his dashboard with written directions to his office. This happened about the same time the paranoia settled in. It was her fault. It had to be her fault—he had done nothing wrong. Even during the long darkness when weeks passed without a single coherent phrase, he sometimes glared at her and said, "How could you do this to me?"

Poetry by Roxie Bulen

I wish I had known . . .

I wish I had known what questions to ask long before
my dad had passed from our world into another.
The belongings he left were so few
they fit into a single box,
yet spoke of a life I never really knew.

Among his treasures an old flight log
with the last entry in '56, the year of my birth,
penned with his familiar left-handed slant
lying next to his private pilot's license.

He was born the oldest with a sense of responsibility,
a big brother with compassion and wisdom,
and then a soldier with patriotic pride and courage.

He came home from his duty a young man with hopes and
        dreams,
dreams to soar through the skies.
Dreams that died before they could take root in the
        conscious mind
like the ones that escape in the moments before sunrise.

Responsibility soared instead with each new child,
leaving him to work in the mines with uncertain futures
then moving to the cities with hope anew.

The hope met with destruction at each new corner,
destruction that weakened the ties
within the stronghold of the home.

Left broken, alone, with the roots upended,
the miles and years increased the distance.
Birthday cards and holiday chats were all that remained
of a family once filled with dreams.

Until age began to take its toll and arms began to open.
The circle was nearing completion,
we were beginning again until death unexpectedly shut the
        door.
The Air Force Honor Guard folds the flag while

I wish I had known
the day I was born
how badly he wanted to fly.

Creative Nonfiction by Carol Joan Campbell

The Guest Book

When my husband and I moved into our first house, my Mom gave us a beautiful Guest Book. An 8" X 11" book with a heavy wood cover and back. The front is carved very ornately with flowers and flourishes, and in the middle is carved *Gast Bok*. On the back it says *Made In Sweden*. We're a Scandinavian family, and perhaps the last American generation where I can say I'm 100 percent Swedish and proud of it. All of my grandparents came here from Sweden, with hopes that future generations would live a good life in America, and were proud to be here. How difficult it must have been to leave their homeland, family and friends, but they did so with their folks' and God's blessing, reaching for opportunities and also reaching for the stars.

We used this Guest Book the first time we had the family over and we could serve them a good meal in our new home. Everyone signed it, wishing us health and happiness as we started our lives together. That was over fifty-five years ago. Now it has become a history book, one filled with memories of special occasions including family and friends.

We both were fortunate to have most of our family living in the same town as we did. While growing up, I had all of my grandparents, aunts, uncles, and cousins living within a fifteen mile radius of us, one as close as half a block away. My cousins were playmates, my aunts and uncles like second parents. A good life, filled with many rich memories.

We lived in our first home for fifteen years, and the notes and signatures in the Guest Book increased by many pages. We next moved to a smaller community, but only twenty miles farther south. Still close enough to keep in contact with family and friends. At times when our kids looked through the Guest Book, they would say "I can't believe how many times you've had your same friends sign this book." My answer was always the same. "Isn't it wonderful that we've continued to be friends?"

We completed raising our children in that home until they were married and another generation began. Soon the book held signatures of in-laws and their families. Then some of the signatures began to be sprawling printed names of toddler grandchildren, and then signatures of their boyfriends and girlfriends. Ongoing history.

Now it had become a beloved reading book. Filled with joy, yet sometimes filled with sadness. On the first page, there are ten signatures; however, only two of those loved ones are still alive. Now there is hardly a page where there aren't some who are no longer with us. Still, each page conjures up memories, some laced with sadness, but most continue to instill a wonderful joy in my heart. We make new friends and fill more pages.

I think especially about one entry. My Mom, Dad, sisters, and their families were over, celebrating Christmas Eve in the Swedish tradition, lots of food, snacks, games, lots of laughing and having fun. Mom's health had taken a turn for the worse, and she was walking with a walker now. Still she was joining in with as much laughter as everyone. We finally said our goodbyes, which meant more minutes devoted to conversation and laughs. Everyone chuckled when Mom sat down and I helped her put her boots on. She said, "Doesn't seem so long ago that you were the one sitting down while I put your boots on." What fun we'd all had.

On Christmas morning, I was preparing dinner for my husband's family who were spending Christmas Day with us. The phone rang; it was my sister. Mom had died. She and Dad had gone over to my sister's for Christmas Brunch, but when she got home, she couldn't get out of the car. Dad called an ambulance and she was rushed to the hospital, but she was gone within a half hour.

With many family members close for support, we got through the next few days. Strange though, at times of sorrow, a formerly minute item can become ever so large. I thought of the Guest Book. I hadn't passed it around on Christmas Eve. I felt an overwhelming sorrow that Mom hadn't signed it one more time. I took out the book and lovingly fingered the pages, just to be filled with more love. Then I saw my Mom's final entry made a few months before.

> *Your home is so beautiful. I am sitting in your living room watching the beautiful sunset. Your dinner was scrumptious. When I reach the realm up above, I hope to look down on this happy group and hope you have taken care of all the wishes in our well—but right now, I know we will be here for a long time. Thanks, kids. It's always fun to all be together.*
>
> *(Signed) Mom and Dad.*

Undoubtedly, God knew more about what was ahead than Mom did. I no longer felt that I had missed having her sign one last time.

Honorable Mention Poetry by Anne M. Dunn

The Shape of Death

My mother said
Grandfather wanted to see me.
Grandmother took me on the streetcar
To a hospice where pale-faced nuns
Robed black as widows
Fretted over the dying.

Emaciated beyond recognition,
Grandfather wore the shape of death.
I would not kiss him,
But held his withered hand.
Tears sparked in kindly eyes
That saw the other shore.
Quickly he released me
Lest he carry me away.

I almost never recall
That shape of death.
But see him tall and strong,
Dancing down the road far ahead of me,
A long bow coaxing music
From a fiddle tucked under his chin.

"The talking stick is a Native American tradition used to facilitate an orderly discussion. The stick is made of wood, decorated with feathers or fur, beads or paint, or a combination of all. Usually speakers are arranged in a talking circle and the stick is passed from hand to hand as the discussion progresses. It encourages all to speak and allows each person to speak without interruption. The talking stick brings all natural elements together to guide and direct the talking circle."

--Anne M. Dunn

This year, we received 324 submissions from 165 writers, by far the most ever received. The editorial board selected 94 poems, 19 creative nonfiction, and 18 fiction pieces from 112 writers for inclusion in this volume.

Thank you for your support!
Visit us at:
www.thetalkingstick.com
www.jackpinewriters.com